The Ink of the Scholars

This book is a translation of Souleymane Bachir Diagne's *L'encre des savants : réflexions sur la philosophie en Afrique* published in 2013 by CODESRIA (Dakar) and Présence Africaine Éditions (Paris).

The Ink of the Scholars

Reflections on Philosophy in Africa

Souleymane Bachir Diagne

Translated from French by
Jonathan Adjemian

CODESRIA

Council for the Development of Social Science Research in Africa
DAKAR

© CODESRIA 2016
Council for the Development of Social Science Research in Africa
Avenue Cheikh Anta Diop, Angle Canal IV
P.O. Box 3304 Dakar, CP 18524, Senegal
Website: www.codesria.org

ISBN: 978-2-86978-705-6

Typesetting: Daouda Thiam
Cover Design: Ibrahima Fofana

Distributed in Africa by CODESRIA
Distributed elsewhere by African Books Collective, Oxford, UK
Website: www.africanbookscollective.com

The Council for the Development of Social Science Research in Africa (CODESRIA) is an independent organisation whose principal objectives are to facilitate research, promote research-based publishing and create multiple forums geared towards the exchange of views and information among African researchers. All these are aimed at reducing the fragmentation of research in the continent through the creation of thematic research networks that cut across linguistic and regional boundaries.

CODESRIA publishes *Africa Development*, the longest standing Africa based social science journal; *Afrika Zamani*, a journal of history; the *African Sociological Review*; the *African Journal of International Affairs*; *Africa Review of Books* and the *Journal of Higher Education in Africa*. The Council also co-publishes the *Africa Media Review*; *Identity, Culture and Politics: An Afro-Asian Dialogue*; *The African Anthropologist, Journal of African Tranformation, Méthod(e)s: African Review of Social Sciences Methodology*, and the *Afro-Arab Selections for Social Sciences*. The results of its research and other activities are also disseminated through its Working Paper Series, Green Book Series, Monograph Series, Book Series, Policy Briefs and the *CODESRIA Bulletin*. Select CODESRIA publications are also accessible online at www.codesria.org

CODESRIA would like to express its gratitude to the Swedish International Development Cooperation Agency (SIDA), the International Development Research Centre (IDRC), the Ford Foundation, the Carnegie Corporation of New York (CCNY), the Norwegian Agency for Development Cooperation (NORAD), the Danish Agency for International Development (DANIDA), the Netherlands Ministry of Foreign Affairs, the Rockefeller Foundation, the Open Society Foundations (OSFs), TrustAfrica, UNESCO, UN Women, the African Capacity Building Foundation (ACBF) and the Government of Senegal for supporting its research, training and publication programmes.

Table of Contents

Preface

"The Ink of the Scholars is more precious than the blood of the martyrs" is a saying from Prophet Muhammad (pbuh) that gives its title to this book. Ahmad Bâba, arguably the most famous scholar from Timbuktu, quotes that statement and makes it the heart of his work *On the Merits of Scholars,* a reflection on the importance of the pursuit and the transmission of knowledge. Such a title can certainly serve as an emblem for his hometown, as Timbuktu was, historically, an intellectual beacon, an important center of learning and written erudition.

So the title "the Ink of the Scholars", being a reference to a work on *The Merits of Scholars* by a scholar from Timbuktu is meant to shift the focus from the usual discussion about orality and oral tradition to the consideration of a tradition of written erudition which is very important, still to be studied further, and an integral part of the reflection on philosophy in Africa,

But of course this title plays another crucial role given the current context prevailing in certain regions of Africa, in particular in northern Mali, where Timbuktu came under attack from terrorist groups who loathe what the old monuments and the ancient manuscripts in that city stand for: the love for humanity and its creations, the spirit of tolerance that comes with knowledge and wisdom. At a time when terrorists attack institutions of learning and express hatred for education and the pursuit of a knowledge they absurdly call "western", it may be useful to recall that the very religion in the name of which they pretend to be allowed to take so many innocent lives with their own proclaims loud and clear that the only combat that can be deemed holy is the one for the enlightenment of knowledge, for the appropriation of the word of wisdom whatever its origin: the ink of the scholars is more precious than the blood of the martyrs.

Acknowledgements

This English translation of the original text in French was sponsored by the Institute of African Studies at Columbia. I thank its Director Mamadou Diouf for his continuous support. I also express my gratitude to Jinny Prais, the Deputy Director of the Institute, and to Jonathan Adjemian who first translated part of the text as a reading for one of his classes before offering to complete the work. Ebrima Sall, the Executive Secretary of CODESRIA is the one who asked me to write these "Reflections on Philosophy in Africa". I am grateful to him for the great support I received from CODESRIA and from him personally.

Introduction

The year 1996 was the fourth centennial of the birth of René Descartes, considered, as we all know, the father of modern philosophy. Quite naturally, the Association des Sociétés de Philosophie de Langue Française (Association of French-Language Philosophy Societies or ASPLF), decided to mark this anniversary by making the 26th International Conference of Philosophy an important colloquium on the topic of 'the Cartesian Spirit'.[1] Also quite naturally, the prestigious Sorbonne provided the event with the use of rooms and amphitheatres. I was accorded the honour of giving a plenary address in one of these amphitheatres. I presented a reflection that was titled 'Cartesian spirit and mathematics of the spirit', concerned on the one hand with Cartesian algebra, and on the other with algebra of logic, in its Leibnizian and then Boolean forms.[2] The questions and commentaries that followed were what would be expected, given the subject, until someone – an African – spoke from the balcony: 'Bachir', he asked me, 'in your university, in Dakar, or anywhere else in Africa, would you have treated this same conference topic in the same way?'

The question elicited several disapproving reactions, as the audience understood it as an accusation: I had 'forgotten' to speak of Descartes, the respondent seemed to say, from my position as an *African* philosopher, from my *difference*, and on the contrary had installed myself comfortably *among* Descartes, Leibniz and Boole, at the heart of a history of philosophy and mathematics tacitly agreed upon as *ours*, all of us, since those in the amphitheatre shared the *same identity* as these philosophers. Although they may have believed that in showing what they thought of the question they were defending me from an inappropriate accusation, those who made murmurs of disapproval were committing a perhaps inevitable misinterpretation of the question's intent. What was the respondent *really* asking? Knowing that the speaker was none other than the Beninese philosopher Paulin Hountondji already indicates that he was not proposing some kind of duty to speak on a subject with a title along the lines of 'Descartes from an African perspective' or 'Cartesian spirit and African thought'. Among Paulin Hountondji's central theses, as we know, an important place is given to the assertion that African philosophy, in the final analysis, is simply the totality of philosophical texts written by philosophers who *happen to be* Africans. My own understanding was that Paulin Hountondji wanted *both* my presentation to be as it was *and* the discussion that followed it to be an opportunity to address the fact that a discussion of 'the Cartesian spirit' (which is often considered to be the spirit of European modernity itself) can also provide an opportunity to evoke traditions of thought from *elsewhere*. I recall that my response to Hountondji's friendly and provocative interpellation followed these lines.[3]

What his question really meant to say was several things. The first is something the philosopher Catherine Malabou expressed when responding to the question of whether she could simply ignore her situation as a woman while writing philosophy. 'How can one', she asked in response to this question, 'appropriate, just like that, the protocols, techniques and symbols of a discourse and of a culture for which one has been, for centuries, the zero point?'[4] What Catherine Malabou says here about being a woman philosopher is also what Hountondji's interpellation, addressed to an African philosopher, says. Yes, there should be Africans present in discussing all the important questions, those of the history of philosophy among others, but this does not mean that it is simple for them to place themselves inside the *same*, in the sense of *identical*, common history, 'just like that'. Then there is also the awareness that the 'discourse' and 'culture' of which Catherine Malabou speaks have, for centuries, often represented its 'zero point' with the features of the African.

Generally speaking, philosophers, who, as Roger-Pol Droit has most aptly put it, 'are tasked, in Western culture, with guarding the great divisions (between true and false, being and nothingness, just and unjust, same and other)', are those who have carried out an initial great 'division between "the self" and "the rest"', between a humanity of the *logos* and the *barbarians*.[5] Outside of this humanity to whom the *logos* has been confided there is then nothing but the 'zero points' of a philosophy which, if it is to remain itself, must always keep them out of the realm of thought, like Descartes who closed the door of his heated room on the disparate, variegated world, lacking foundation in reason, so as to better apply his attention to eternal truths. Similarly, Kant insisted on 'purity' in matters of moral philosophy, which must be carefully and completely cleaned of all empirical elements, since these could only belong to its outside, that is to anthropology. When Kant left off thinking in philosophy in order to wander about in anthropology, in the 'geography' of peoples and of their cultures, we know that he in fact held opinions of 'the others' that were unworthy of the thinker who gave the categorical imperative its well-known sublime formulations.

Nonetheless, it is important not to simplify and to give the image of a history of Western philosophy (which is to say first of all in Greek, then in Latin, then in European languages) as continuously and forever constituting itself through the gesture of excluding other 'humanities' from philosophical reflection. This would be to forget that the Greeks themselves did not claim to be the inventors of philosophy,[6] or that Descartes declared without hesitation that algebra, with all that it offers to thought, came, as its name indicates, from Arabic-speaking foreigners. In truth, European philosophy's closure on itself became a reality mainly in the eighteenth and nineteenth centuries. Roger-Pol Droit, who emphasizes this point, looks for the reasons of what appears to him as a 'reduction of the field of application of the term "philosophy"' in the way that philosophers understand their discipline.[7] Undoubtedly, the question of what the term 'philosophy' covers is important when asking whether, for example, Indian, Chinese, or Sufi spiritualities, and so on, are philosophy. But above all and first of all, the 'civilizing missions' that the European colonial powers held themselves to be invested in imposed a great division separating the 'rest' from a Europe, carrier in its very essence of that highest manifestation of spirit, philosophy, in which those who were destined to be Europeanized through colonization, allowing their *mentality* to be transmuted into thought, could not therefore have participated. Prior to semantic considerations, the question of 'philosophies from elsewhere' is unavoidably tied to the colonial situation and to its translation into ethnological discourse on an 'elsewhere' that could never be philosophical without contradiction.

But why, first of all, should the philosophers of exclusion whom Roger-Pol Droit evokes be granted the privilege of defining the 'field of application' of the word 'philosophy' and of closing it in on itself, onto what was invented in the nineteenth century as the unique trajectory of a European humanity born only from itself and developing only by its own *telos*? In other words, why shouldn't the philosophies developed in other human societies write themselves, without referring to the status of 'zero point' that a certain colonial gaze has given them? When discussing philosophy in Africa then, it is necessary to examine this intellectual history – which largely remains to be written-, asking what it has been and what are its most important aspects.

How does philosophy present itself in Africa? To speak of 'philosophies from elsewhere' raises the question of what philosophy is, but the question of the meaning of the word 'Africa' must also be posed. Should the Sahara be considered to divide two worlds, the Arab-Berber and the Black? Or, pushing the divisions further, should the continent be considered to be fragmented into innumerable cultural territories, so that it is impossible to characterize any given (art, religion, etc.) as *African*, since the discourse that is valid for a given territory ceases to be so beyond its borders? In a curious see-saw movement, discourse on the continent has passed from careless generalizations concerning an Africanity everywhere identical to the scrupulous juxtaposition, to the point of absurdity, of territorial singularities impossible to subsume under *one* notion of Africa. So, in spite of undeniable family resemblances, one ends up saying, like Picasso but with a completely different meaning from his own: '*African* art? Never heard of it!'

So then, Africa? In an interview published in 2008, the Congolese philosopher Valentin Y. Mudimbe remarked that his book *The Invention of Africa* is precisely based on the question: 'What is Africa? And what do we understand by "Africa" when we use the term?' Mudimbe explains:

> To pose the question is to give place to semantic distinctions that impose themselves surreptitiously. So we have North Africa, Saharan Africa, Sub-Saharan Africa and Southern Africa. Categories of a linguistic order are sometimes used to determine a different geography in which can notably be distinguished Arabophone Africa, Anglophone Africa, Lusophone Africa, and Francophone Africa.[9]

As far as these latter linguistic categories are concerned, it is clear that they pose the problem of the other languages spoken on the continent, which find themselves marginalized: the different Berber dialects and the African languages that are sometimes called 'endogenous'. And as for the first sequence of divisions, we know what kind of 'philosophical' justifications they were given in Hegel's *Lessons on the Philosophy of History*.

Geography, according to Hegel, has a crucial importance for the history of the Spirit, and most important of all is for a land to be penetrated throughout by water and so to be open to the infinity of the sea, which is none other than that of the Spirit. So Hegel believed he could tell from the map where a continent's identity gives itself to be read, that Africa is a mass folded in on itself and closed up into a veritable night of the Spirit, like the oblivion of sleep. So on the map he detached from what he called 'Africa proper' on the one hand, Egypt which he attached to Asia, and on the other, the Maghreb, whose outline manifested its destiny to extend to Europe by becoming its colony. One of the consequences Hegel drew from these hurried considerations about Africa (and what little there is to say about it should, he suggested, be said quickly and never returned to) was that slavery, specifically that of the triangular trade, which was certainly an evil in itself, nonetheless could represent an exit from the night of the Spirit; this commerce of humans opened up the possibility for Africans of seeing their intelligence and talents blossom in a more favourable theatre. And, to illustrate this point, Hegel cited the case of an African doctor who, placed in the radically different conditions of the New World, was noted as the inventor of a medicine against a certain illness.

Two remarks will be made here. The first one is prompted by the evocation of slavery, which adds a supplementary dimension to the question 'What is Africa?', because the creation of diasporic populations of African origins in the New World also means that Africa is not only in Africa. This is also what the African Union affirmed when it took the symbolic decision of adding a sixth African region, that of the diaspora, to the five 'regions' of the continent which are understood to be on the path to becoming spaces integrated along cultural, social, economic and political lines. And, concerning philosophy, the concept of *Africana Philosophy*, where the Latin *africana* at once translates a continental and a diasporic Africanity, aims to give substance to a certain continuity and community between the two.[10]

The second remark concerns the consequence of this Hegelian partition of Africa, which is precisely that it impedes the task of understanding the continent's intellectual history. To cut off North Africa from sub-Saharan Africa is to make the Sahara into a wall that it never has been, transforming this space into a border, or worse into an uncrossable barrier, when on the contrary it has always been open and traversed by various flows: human, commercial, intellectual. The Islamization of a large part of sub-Saharan Africa, in particular, is in direct relation to the existence of commercial networks that linked this region to Mediterranean Africa and, extending further, to the rest of the Muslim world. These networks from then on could not avoid becoming routes of transmission for Islamic knowledge as well. This is attested to by the important centres of teaching that developed, for example in West Africa (also called *Bilâd as-Sudân*, 'the country of the Blacks', or simply *Sudân*) under the Mali and Songhay empires. The legendary city of Timbuktu, commercial crossroads of trans-Saharan routes, is undoubtedly the paragon of these centres.[11] Timbuktu today is a witness and a symbol that reminds us of an important fact too often ignored when it comes to the question of the intellectual history of Africa and, in particular, of African philosophy: it is simply not true that African cultures are in their essence oral cultures. Before reducing the question of philosophy in Africa into that of an African 'oral reason',[12] it is necessary, first of all, to take full consideration of what was written and taught in the philosophical disciplines in Africa, for example in the field of logic in the Aristotelian tradition, long before the arrival of the school that would be qualified as 'European'. The history of philosophical thought in Africa, yesterday as today, and as it is everywhere, is a history of encounters. As Séverine Kodjo Grandvaux writes:

> African philosophies ceaselessly deterritorialize and reterritorialize philosophies and concepts that are foreign to them, and construct themselves as an encounter.[13]

All these questions have been evoked because they unavoidably present themselves as so many aspects of the general problem of 'African philosophizing'. We will, therefore, not be able to avoid examining them as we proceed, but will not dwell on them too much here. The present work is meant mostly as a 'memento' or a 'précis' of philosophical activity in Africa. This means first of all that it makes no claims to be exhaustive on the subject, although it aims, of course, to shed light on its essential aspects. This also means that we will not exhaust ourselves in prolegomena on the naturally interminable question of what deserves to be called African philosophy. As movement is proved by walking, we simply need to point out that in several universities today, mainly American ones admittedly, a programme of teaching African or *Africana* philosophy exists[14] and is increasingly developing in importance, which translates into increasingly numerous publications, which include important reference works.[15] The best point of departure, therefore, is to lay out a field of questions, a sphere of debate that could be called 'African' or 'Africana', revolving around issues such as three proposed by Lewis Gordon that we consider essential for that sphere: philosophical anthropology, philosophy of liberation and the meta-critical evaluation of reason.[16]

So it seemed to me that a good way to proceed, corresponding to my hope of providing a *précis*, was to consider the following four major questions:

1. The question of a philosophy of life force and of aesthetic discourse. This involves examining the idea that the African religions called traditional, as distinct from Christianity and Islam, religions of the book, are based on a particular ontology of vital forces that is also expressed in the different artistic traditions found on the continent.

2. The question of time and of prospective in relation to African languages. This involves analysing the controversy which divided philosophers into those who believed they could infer an African conception of time concrete and without a true future dimension from the ways calendars and tenses are expressed in certain African languages, from other philosophers who say exactly the opposite on the basis of considerations from other African languages.

3. The question of orality and of writing in relation to philosophical thought.

4. The question of political thought, and in particular the way in which African socialisms have been presented as doctrines that are at once rooted in a certain African philosophy of community and are carriers of a modernity in which the continent can find the path towards its development. This question leads naturally to that of human rights and of democracy in Africa.

The Force of Living[17]

If my theory is correct, everything that has been written up till now on ethnology, and all that will be written in the future, will need to find its deepest base and its highest complement in the philosophy of forces.

Placide Tempels (Letter to Husltaert)[18]

Bantu Philosophy: A Contradictory Text

Bantu Philosophy,[19] by the Reverend Father Placide Tempels, can be considered one of the pioneering works that made so-called 'African' philosophy a question of importance for philosophical reflection in general. When it was published in 1949, the book was at first welcomed eagerly by many African intellectuals. Léopold Sédar Senghor quickly declared it indispensable for any library worth the name, and Alioune Diop hailed it, in the preface he wrote, as the most important work written to date about Africa: the book was essential for Black people, he declared, and equally so for anyone who wanted to understand Africans.[20] We know the reason for the enthusiasm that Senghor and Alioune Diop expressed, along with Cheikh Anta Diop and many others: thanks to Fr. Placide Tempels and the title of his book, 'African philosophy' was no longer an oxymoron.

Bantu Philosophy thus gave an example of the task to be accomplished if one was a philosopher and an African. Many reflections would be published, following its model, on the philosophy or thought of this or that people, or on African 'spirit' or 'thought' in general. In fact, the adjective 'Bantu' was considered by many, explicitly or implicitly, as a synecdoche for 'African'. Evidently, this was not without its problems as we will see later.

Next, the book became a target for the iconoclastic fury of a subsequent generation of African intellectuals. True, these thinkers could claim that they were only extending and amplifying the instinctive defiance and scepticism of another of their elders, Aimé Césaire, who had not foregone the opportunity, immediately and in contrast to his friend Senghor, to turn his sarcasm on this Belgian missionary who himself confessed that his desire to understand 'Bantu philosophy' had the additional goal of saving the colonial order. Revolts were becoming more and more perceptible and organized, and were led by people whom Tempels considered to be pseudo- *'évolués'*,[21] uprooted people in his eyes, displaced and therefore to be mistrusted: trouble-makers in their very being. Prolonging Césaire's scepticism, there emerged a radical, 'theoretical' critique of the work in the 1970s: this Bantu philosophy, and all the other philosophies it had given birth to – Wolof, Akan, Yoruba and others – would need to be stored where they belonged: on the shelves of the ethnological literature and its ethno-philosophical appendages, so that the African intellectual landscape would not find itself upside-down in a total confusion of genres. So that 'true' African philosophy would be possible, and produced by authors taking individual responsibility for their theses, arguments and propositions.

Before examining these contradictory evaluations, we should remember one fact and make one clarification. The fact is that *Bantu Philosophy* is, today, simply an important book, the one that marked the beginning of African philosophy[22] as an academic discipline taught from then on in the best philosophy departments, that is to say the ones in which a received idea is being put in question: that of philosophy as the history of a unique spirit whose geography happens naturally to correspond to that of a Greek, Latin, Christian, modern, and finally, contemporary Europe. At the end of the Second World War, as decolonizations announced themselves in the fractures of an imperialism that could no longer be confident in itself, this book put forward the question of African philosophizing and of its proper modes of existence.

The clarification is that, in truth, this book by Father Tempels was not the first book of its kind, nor the first to be concerned with the philosophy of Bantu peoples. We could recall, for example, the work of the British subject William Vernon Brelsford who found himself in 1930, at age twenty-three, a functionary in Northern Rhodesia, after failing the Indian Civil Service exam that would have opened the doors to a more prestigious colonial career in the country that was known as the jewel of the Crown. Having decided to make the best of his situation, Brelsford started by taking interest in the purification rites practised by certain local populations, and then published a more theoretical work on *Primitive Philosophy* in 1935. The English gentleman had fired first, but probably not hit on a good title. Choosing the adjective 'primitive' diluted the import of the word 'philosophy'. One can hardly help but think 'mentality' in its place. To the contrary, associating 'philosophy' with the 'Bantu', a specific group of African peoples,[23] had a wholly different weight. Here an African subject, even if a collective one, was declared to be the carrier of a philosophical system.

Aimé Césaire's *Discourse on Colonialism*, that merciless indictment of colonialism, was clearly not the place for Tempels, 'missionary and Belgian', to be granted any mercy in Césaire's eyes, or for his *Bantu philosophy* to be seen as anything more than a work 'as slimy and fetid as one could wish', with its only goal being 'to counteract the "communistic materialism" which, it seems, threatens to turn the Negroes into "moral vagabonds".'[24] Césaire exempted himself from the task of criticizing, that is to say of examining, what Father Tempels had to say: he dismissed it out of hand.

Césaire had every reason to denounce the project of analysing *Bantu Philosophy* as eminently political. At the time the work was written, it was becoming more and more obvious that the colonial order could not continue to exist in the way it had. Europe could no longer pretend to be dealing with a primitive humanity naturally inclined to be led, and which, on the subjects of being, the human, truth, knowledge, beauty, justice, et cetera, had nothing to say. Possoz, who wrote a preface to Tempels' work dated 20 July 1945, identified its principal merit as marking a new era in colonial history: colonizing Europe recognized its 'previous ethnological errors' and understood that it now needed to pay attention to what 'the others' might be *thinking*. In his preface to the edition published by Présence Africaine, Alioune Diop also wrote:

> For centuries now [Europe] has only looked into the mirror of its own consciousness, condemning itself never to know itself, to know life only incompletely, because it deprived the others ... of the Gaze, of the Speech, which might have led to the capture and revelation of the Destiny of Humanity.[25]

Fr. Tempels himself clearly indicated the political import of his book:

> The fact is that those in high positions do not know which patron saint to turn to for guidance in directing the Bantu, There is less than ever any stable native politics, and ... we come up short in the matter of providing secure and trustworthy directives to ensure the evolution and civilization of the Bantu.[26]

It was therefore necessary to teach those whom the colonial situation had put in the situation of 'living among the natives' how to 'understand the Bantu', to make themselves 'intelligible to them' and to know how to avoid, 'while believing that one is "civilizing" the individual ... in fact corrupting him, working to increase the numbers of the deracinated and becoming the architect of revolts'.[27]

For 'revolts' there were.[28] They were for the most part the works of those '*évolués*' who, in the Belgian missionary's emphatic view, constituted the very symptom of a colonialism in the process of turning against itself.

Furthermore, nothing better translates the inequality, the essential asymmetry constitutive of the colonial relationship, than the missionary's declaration, made early and presented as self-evident, that there can be no question of imagining for a second that the *Muntu* himself – the Bantu subject – could, in some fashion, lay out the ontological system of which his most fundamental attitudes, his way of being in the world, are the expression. For this he needed to wait for the White Man, and offered himself to a colonization and naturally also an evangelization that would fulfil the promise that his philosophy carried. But when, later on, Fr. Tempels asks, concerning the Bantu, 'is their wisdom critical?', this is not simply a rhetorical question that he would be expected to answer with a definitive 'no'. In fact – and this was his justification for choosing to use the word 'philosophy' with regard to the Bantu instead of the more neutral, more watered-down notions of 'worldview', 'thought' or 'wisdom' – the missionary held the opposite view: if the philosophy of forces impregnates and 'penetrates their understanding as a whole' rather than appearing clearly to them as 'a field of play for the reasoning of a rational critical philosophy', nonetheless the requirement of being founded on 'observation of reality and on deductions which can be drawn from human experience' is present in it, and this makes 'Bantu philosophy ... a critical philosophy as rightly so called as our western systems'.[29]

Lucien Lévy-Bruhl, in order to reassure and comfort a European self-identity as rational, logical and philosophic, had concocted for the 'others' a 'primitive' and 'prelogical' mentality, unaware of the principle of contradiction and the law of causality. Although it does not mention it by name, it is clearly this prelogicality put forward by the French philosopher–ethnologist that *Bantu Philosophy* refutes.[30] It is important to insist on the importance of this refutation, and to further clarify the general philosophical stakes by considering it alongside other refutations of Lévy-Bruhl's kind of ethnology in the 1930s from the pens of Henri Bergson and Ludwig Wittgenstein.[31]

The basics of Bergson's lesson can be found in passages in *The Two Sources of Morality and Religion* where he dismisses the thesis of prelogicality that Lévy-Bruhl believed he had established by starting from the idea that the primitive was indifferent to secondary causes, and always explained by means of a 'mystical' cause phenomena that healthy reason has taught us (that is to say: we, the non-primitive humanity) to ascribe to invariable natural principles. Bergson ultimately declares that the inference according to which the 'savage' is unaware of the relation between a cause and its effect is itself illogical. To begin with, it is contradictory since everything in the comportment of a human who relies 'on the current of the river to carry his canoe ... on the bending of his bow to shoot his arrow, on his hatchet to cut into the trunk, on his teeth to bite, on his legs to walk' indicates that he is perfectly conscious of what is meant by the invariability of natural laws.[32] It is worth citing Bergson's important lines at length:

> When the primitive man turns to a mystic cause for the explanation of death, illness or any other accident, what exactly is the process that he goes through? He sees, for instance, that a man has been killed by a fragment of rock dislodged during a gale. Does he deny that the rock was already split, that the wind loosened the stone, that the blow cracked the skull? Obviously not. He notes, as we do, the operation of these proximate causes. Why then, does he bring in a 'mystic cause', such as the will of a spirit or witch-doctor, to set it up as the principal cause? Let us look closer: we shall see that what the primitive man explains here as a 'supernatural' cause is not the physical effect, it is its *human significance*, it is its importance to man, and more especially to a particular man, the one who was crushed by the stone. There is nothing illogical, consequently nothing 'prelogical' or even anything which evinces an 'imperviousness to experience', in the belief that a cause should be proportionate to its effect, that, once having admitted the crack in the rock, the direction and force of the wind – purely physical things which take no account of

humanity – there remains to be explained this fact so momentous to us: the death of a man. The effect is contained pre-eminently in the cause, as the old philosophers used to put it; and if the effect has a considerable human significance, the cause must have at least an equal significance; it is in any case of the same order: it is an *intention*.[33]

What Bergson reminds us is that the principle of sufficient reason is always present and readable, even in the recourse to a 'mystical cause'. Such an appeal is, the philosopher says, an 'operation' that entirely obeys the principle of reason that demands that we make cause and effect proportionate, that as Descartes says there 'at least be as much reality in the efficient and total cause as in its effect: for whence can the effect draw its reality if not from its cause?'[34] If a human death has taken place, since no human could possibly die simply by chance, from a gust of wind and a crack in a rock, then there is something here that does not add up for *our* reason, the search for meaning we share in common, all of us human animals who know that we will die. The invocation of an 'intention' answers precisely this question of meaning. Other responses, surely, are possible and might have more validity for reason, or might claim to be more satisfying. But that does not contradict this first response as long as all of them address, in the same way 'intention' does, the *same question* which constitutes our human condition. That condition is what Bergson stresses here against the idea of separate humanities implied in the notion of a 'primitive mentality', showing, by means of specific examples, that this mentality is also shared by the 'civilized', who can no longer claim a monopoly on 'logic'.

To an ethnology so impatiently eager to manufacture otherness, or the radically other, Bergson administers a lesson in logic and simple good sense, founded on a humanist principle – that nothing another human does is foreign to me – which it in turn verifies. This is the same lesson, articulated in similar terms, by the *Remarks* that Frazer's *Golden Bough* inspired Ludwig Wittgenstein to note down around 1930.

Jacques Bouveresse has perceptively declared of Wittgenstein that 'we could say, in a certain way, and on the condition of understanding his true objective, that he was never concerned with anything but anthropology'.[35] Quoting paragraph 206 of his *Philosophical Investigations*, where Wittgenstein states that 'the common behavior of mankind is the system of reference by means of which we interpret an unknown language',[36] Bouveresse writes that 'to abstract from this minimal system of reference would be to treat someone who we consider in the abstract to be human as if he had nothing human about him', and evokes the remark, once again commonsense, that the logician W.V. Quine had made about the supposed prelogicity of 'primitive mentality'. Considering what he admitted was surely a 'caricature' or an 'extreme simplification' of Lévy-Bruhl's thesis, Quine wrote:

> Let us suppose it claimed that these natives accept as true a certain sentence of the form 'p and not p. Or—not to oversimplify too much—that they accept as true a certain heathen sentence of the form 'q ka bu q' the English translation of which has the form 'p and not p'. But now just how good a translation is this, and what may the lexicographer's method have been? If any evidence can count against a lexicographer's adoption of 'and' and 'not' as translations of 'ka' and 'bu', certainly the natives' acceptance of 'q ka bu q' as true counts overwhelmingly. We are left with the meaninglessness of the doctrine of there being pre-logical peoples; pre-logicality is a trait injected by bad translators.[37]

Wittgenstein makes the same point when he reproaches Frazer for ignoring what is at the very base of a relation between different cultures or 'forms of life': attention to what the other is really saying, which itself rests on the ethical orientation of translation, described by Antoine Berman[38] as an orientation towards the humanity I know to be in front of me in the signs that I learn to decipher, and which expresses genuine attention to what is familiar to me in the other. The differentialist posture, which betrays the ethnographer's initial conviction that he is dealing with an *other* way of being that is so foreign to him that it could hold 'p and not p' as true, does nothing but invent what it is looking for – this same difference, which we accordingly can only 'understand' as shocking and inconsistent. Wittgenstein says that in the end Frazer 'is much more "savage" than most of his savages', as 'his explanations of primitive practices are much cruder than the meaning of these practices themselves'.[39] We should not be surprised that this judgement echoes the question Bergson addressed to Lévy-Bruhl:

> But, to that eminent philosopher we shall say, when you reproach primitive man with not believing in chance, or at least when you state it to be a characteristic trait of his mentality that he does not believe in it, are you not admitting the existence of chance, and in admitting it are you quite sure that you are not relapsing into that primitive mentality you criticize, which at all events you are at great pains to distinguish radically from your own?

These logical refutations by Bergson and Wittgenstein of the ethnographic construction of otherness in the style of Lévy-Bruhl help us better evaluate the significance of *Bantu Philosophy*. This work is at once neocolonial and postcolonial in the way that it treats the question of translation. We can refer to the distinction Antoine Berman makes on this subject: for him, essentially, there is a form of translation that 'gives in to [an] appropriational and reductive injunction, and forms itself as one of its agents', leading to 'ethnocentric translations, or what we may call "bad" translations'. What is 'by its very nature opposed to this injunction' is then 'the *ethical aim* of translation'. 'The essence of translation is to be an opening, a dialogue, a *métissage*, a decentering. Translation is putting in touch, or it is *nothing*.'[40]

We can say that these two aspects coexist, in contradiction, within *Bantu Philosophy*. It is the 'appropriational and reductive injunction' that leads to saying that the *muntu* himself cannot know how to explicitly articulate the philosophy he carries or that is 'deposited' in his language and his ways of seeing the world, and which only the European *subject supposed to know* will be able to *translate*, that is to say explicitly, identify. Translation accordingly is in support of colonial 'governmentality' (to borrow a concept from Michel Foucault), which Aimé Césaire is right to attack. But, on the other hand, there is also a will towards 'putting in touch with', towards dialogue, a will to carry out a translation that would be careful and open. This, too, is in the spirit of the ethnology of the 1930s and 1940s, when Tempels was studying Bantu languages and cultures, as culturalist approaches began to insist on the internal coherence of societies previously considered to be far too 'primitive' for us to expect that we could really 'understand' them.[41] On the contrary, it was in order to understand them from close up, as intimately as possible, that it was necessary, first of all, to go beyond ethnography, beyond ethnology, to an encounter with *philosophy* that is the ultimate abode of meaning, and that is therefore necessary for any 'good' translation. In a letter to Father Hulstaert dated 3 May 1945, Reverend Tempels wrote along these lines that 'to do good ethnology, I believe we need to come to see things from the Bantu point of view'.[42]

Ontology of Living Force

What, then, is the content of the 'Bantu philosophy' that, properly speaking, was dismissed more than it was criticized by Césaire?

In fact, the only moment where the Martinican poet considers the book's contents, is when he sarcastically gives the following 'summary':

> Now then, know that Bantu thought is essentially ontological; that Bantu ontology is based on the truly fundamental notions of a life force and a hierarchy of life forces; and that for the Bantu the ontological order, which defines the world, comes from God and, as a divine decree, must be respected.[43]

Césaire makes a remark after this brief summary of Tempels' presentation that often has not been sufficiently noticed: 'It is clear', he writes in a note at the bottom of the page, 'that I am not attacking

Bantu philosophy here, but the way in which certain people try to use it for political ends'. So then might it be that the content itself – Bantu philosophy itself – may not be invalid, and that the attack is directed only towards the political use that is made of that philosophy? If that is the case, then what is it? Is it something *other* than what Fr. Tempels says it is? It may be that Césaire recognizes, beneath his sarcasm and dismissal, that there is truth in what the Belgian missionary's book describes as being Bantu philosophy, the ontology of vital force presented by him as the key to accessing the mental universe of the Baluba.

Fr. Tempels' book has the rich simplicity of a theory that is entirely centred on one notion, that of *vital force*. This concept is presented as the specific Bantu difference, and, at the same time, as the unique key able to yield up the ultimate meaning of the ways of doing, living, judging and thinking of the populations whose proverbs, songs and legends he had patiently gathered and whose language he had learned. This concept should then be able to be read in other cultural regions, in the cosmic significance of animal sacrifice for the Dogon of Mali, or in the usage of stylization, to the point of abstraction, in African sculpture. In his preface, Alioune Diop underlined that in this book published right at the exit from the horror of the Second World War, vital power found itself re-established in a humanist sense. It was not the will to power's message of death whose diabolical celebration Nazism had represented; on the contrary it was, Diop wrote in a style that shifted to the lyrical when he evoked it, this fullness of life and this fervour to exist that, according to him, constitutes African being-in-the-world.

The philosopher and logician Léo Apostel (1925–95), also a Belgian it should be noted, managed to dissect the philosophical object called 'Bantu philosophy' and to present it as made up of seven (ontological) principles, as follows:

A1: The existence of anything is its being a force, and the essence of anything is its being a force.

A2: Every force is specific.

A3: Different types of beings are characterized by different intensities and types of force.

A4: Each force can be strengthened or weakened.

A5: Forces can influence each other and act upon each other in virtue of their internal natures. All forces are radically interdependent internally.

A6: The universe is a hierarchical order of forces according to their strengths.

A7: Beings occupying a higher rank in the hierarchy can influence all beings of lower rank, at any distance; beings of higher rank can influence beings of lower rank or equal rank, indirectly by using beings of lower rank; beings of equal rank can weaken or strengthen directly and internally the force of another being of equal rank.[44]

Each of these axioms is surrounded by comments clarifying their meaning. So, discussing the first thesis, A1, Apostel recalls that 'the distinction between essence and existence is typical for Aristotelianism and Tempels does not clearly say in so many words that in Africa both essence and existence are force, but we claim that attentive reading of his work compels us to come to this conclusion'. The Belgian logician emphasizes the importance of A2, since it implicitly rejects the identification of 'a 'mana' or 'cosmical force' that would 'penetrate each individual'. On the contrary, each force 'is an undivided and indivisible type of individuality'.[45] There is no pantheism to be found here, Apostel concludes.

Theses A5 and A7, it seems, could be taken to constitute the foundational reason of what is called magical thinking. Thesis A4 is crucial since it leads from the ontology of vital force to the ethics that follow from it, whose basic proposition can be formulated accordingly: 'Act in such a way as to intensify the life force of all "*muntu*" (or of all *muntu* belonging to your group)'.[46] Accordingly, evil is the diminishment of a *muntu*'s living force, good its intensification; and duty translates the obligation of doing good, defined in these terms.[47]

Thesis A6 is considered the quintessence not only of the Bantu religion, but that of Africa in general. Without denying the multiplicity and the variety of religious systems, many researchers have seen a common denominator of the religions of sub-Saharan Africa in the idea of a chain of being-forces, running from God to the mineral, and in a cult of living force. Particularly striking is the work of Louis-Vincent Thomas and René Luneau, who bring together an important number of oral texts which, although coming from very different regions of the continent, show profound convergences.[48] For instance, to take a particularly relevant example, informed by many texts they have allowed to be revealed 'an essential dimension that unifies Black African prayer in the diversity of its expressions and of the circumstances that give rise to it: the fact that it is always a "prayer for life"'.[49]

Languages and Translation

The crucial question to be posed to this 'object', defined in the seven theses with all their different implications, is the one that critics in the 1970s posed to Tempels' work and to the work of others written on the same model.[50] What exactly is it that makes it an expression of a Bantu, or more generally, an African, philosophy?

The question can be split this way: first, what is it that makes it the philosophy *of* the Bantu in general, of all the Bantu, or of all Africans; and second, is it specifically, exclusively, Bantu or African? Does it make sense to say that the Bantu, as such, carry, in the most intimate depths of their ways of seeing and thinking, these theses whose validity they demonstrate in their rituals, proverbs, institutions, languages, et cetera? That they *live* this philosophy of life, but without *knowing* it with the kind of knowledge that requires distance in order to *perceive*? A philosophy to which one *adheres*, literally, without the possibility of questioning it – since there is no *outside* from which one could do this – is no longer a philosophy: such was the substance of the critique of ethno-philosophy. Where Tempels believed he had

21

been able to touch philosophy, the intimate underside of what was described by ethnography, his critics saw precisely the lack of what would constitute philosophy, namely distance.

The inexistence of any distance makes this philosophy 'unanimist': everyone in the group (whatever its size) shares it, because it is sufficient to belong to this group in order to receive one's part of this philosophy simultaneously with the language one speaks or the religion to which one is born.

True, one of the implications of Tempels' thesis is that the Bantu *speak their philosophy in an entirely natural fashion.* Accordingly, he explains, they have an 'ontological tongue'. Their language is not like ours; they speak in a concrete fashion, in words that refer immediately to things themselves. They speak 'realistically' or even 'ontologically'.[51] In an article published by the journal *Présence Africaine* titled 'The study of Bantu languages in the light of Bantu philosophy',[52] the author invited Bantuist linguists, just as he had earlier addressed ethnographers, to find in Bantu philosophy, beneath all their classifications and descriptions, the final causes and the 'inner logic' of the languages they study. Because 'language is wisdom speaking',[53] and because 'it is only by understanding the mentality of Black people that we can arrive at extracting the general structure of their language', Tempels saw in the work of these Bantuist linguists a potential reservoir of proofs that could contribute 'to the verification of the hypothesis he had established'.[54]

Let us pause on this idea of an ontological speech in which the word is the thing, since, in various forms, it would be taken up by a number of African philosophers, in a tendency to fall into what we could call the *illusion of natural abstraction.* This illusion consists in accepting the idea that there are naturally abstract languages, in opposition to which Tempels asserts that the language of the Bantu 'is not like ours'. This idea is confronted in every attempt to analyse an African language in a 'concrete' manner, without remembering that the same operation can just as easily be carried out on a language considered, a priori and without trial, as abstract. To take an example that we will return to later on, the Kenyan philosopher John Mbiti gives many examples to demonstrate that the populations whose religion and philosophy he studies have only a concrete notion of a calendar when they speak in their language of 'milking time' or of 'hot sun', used by the Latuka to designate the month of October. Their division of time, he concludes, is a 'phenomenon calendar' in opposition to the calendars he describes as 'mathematical' or 'numerical' since they are not linked to any concrete phenomena. But it is sufficient, while remaining on the topic of diachrony, to look at the etymologies of 'hour' or 'minute' to see that they have not always had, naturally, the 'numerical' value that we give them today, or that 'Mars', 'June', and 'August' refer to the concrete persons of the Roman God of War, of Junius Brutus, first Consul of Rome, and of the Emperor Augustus. The illusion of natural abstraction leads to *over-analysing* African words as concrete, while neglecting to carry out the same operation on the European word that is being referenced implicitly or explicitly.

In fact, if we continue down this route, there is nothing more concrete than the word 'abstract' itself, whose Latin etymology teaches us that it derives from the perfectly concrete fact of *pulling (tirer; trahere, traire) from (à partir de; ab(s))*: we pull an 'abstract' signification from 'concrete' meaning. Ultimately, then, we do not need to exhaust ourselves demonstrating that African languages are as capable of abstraction as any other; this would be trying to break down an open door. The reason that there are no concrete languages is because there are no abstract ones. All that we find are abstract *uses* of the words of language.

The philosopher Alexis Kagamé pursues, on another level, the kind of linguistification of philosophy invited by Tempels' approach. In 1955, Alexis Kagamé presented a thesis in philosophy, *The Bantu-Rwandan Philosophy of Being*.[55] When later, in 1976, *Présence Africaine* published another work of his called *Comparative Bantu Philosophy*, he indicated in his introduction what Tempels' immense merit had been as a path breaker, but also pointed out where the method of the man he called 'our Pioneer' (with a capital P!) 'had been deficient'.[56] The correct method, according to Kagamé, would consist in choosing a 'determinate cultural zone' along with the particular language spoken there, and to examine and read in it, as well as in other aspects of that culture, 'the philosophical elements' found 'embedded' there, and to avoid relying on aspects that 'depend solely on ethnology'.[57] At root, Kagamé reproached Father Tempels for not having gone far enough along the path he had begun to clear, tunneling beneath ethnology. At the end of this path, Kagamé declared in his 1955 thesis, will be found what he calls 'linguistic-philosophy'.

That philosophy is always at the same time linguistics is an important thesis, one that appears in various forms in the works of African and Africanist philosophers. We can clarify the stakes here by invoking Barbara Cassin's important work showing us the extent to which philosophy is tied to *languages*, and exploring the implications that follow.[58] The coordinator of the *Dictionary of Untranslatables*[59] points out, through the infinite project, in many respects Nietzschean, of testing philosophical concepts against the diversity of human languages, that the words which philosophy uses are *words* first before they are *concepts*. She remarks:

> We evidently escape analytic philosophy whenever we support the idea that our entries in the *Dictionary of Untranslatables* are words, rooted in languages, and not concepts: the untranslatable does not just amount to contextual opacity.[60]

To a language that would see itself as the language of philosophy, it is helpful to oppose this multiplicity, and so to subject it to a deterritorialization that would make it conscious of its inscription in difference.[61] Goethe put it well: we know nothing of our own language if we do not know any other. The philosophical dictionary whose project must then be pursued indefinitely is not one that would give equivalents of the same concept in different languages (themselves evidently also conceptual or 'abstract') but one that deterritorializes the ways of speaking that make use of the word in question, and ultimately leads us to become aware of our condition of living in what Hannah Arendt, cited by Barbara Cassin, calls 'the faltering equivocity of the world'.[62]

By rediscovering sophistic wisdom behind what presents itself as *the* philosophical tradition of the *logos*, inseparably thought and speech, Cassin points to the existence of those whose speech had been evacuated from a philosophy that aimed to be at once universal and monolingual: sophists, women, Africans. Her project, which voids the substance of what Jean-Pierre Lefebvre has called the 'ontological nationalism' of Heidegger's declaration that philosophy had only one language, Greek yesterday and German today,[63] shows clearly what the stakes are for philosophers in Africa of this question of language (or of languages if we add to Greek and German their Indo-European cousins which share with them, in particular, similar uses of the verb 'to be').

In many respects Kagamé declares himself against ontological nationalism, targeting in particular Aristotle's ontology – the extent of whose debt to Greek grammar the African philosopher demonstrated two years before Emile Benvéniste.[64]

Father Tempels' non-Aristotelian approach consisted in opposing the Bantu *dynamic* ontology of living force to Stagiritic ontology, considered as a *static* method of posing the subject/substance and then attributing to it various attributes/predicates. In other writings, particularly in his correspondence, he claimed that Christian theology, before it petrified more or less into the Aristotelian language of attribution, understood the *logos* above all as a life force. On this point, his correspondence with Father Hulstaert is particularly important. A reading of the letters they exchanged presents us with a Father Hulstaert, obstinately Thomistic, for whom force is a predicate of being: first there is being, then force *happens*, thus constituting an accident. It also presents us with a Father Tempels who insists, in turn, on the need to go beyond the way that 'European' language influences us to talk and think, in order to see things like the Bantus: 'For the time being, therefore, make no more Thomistic objections to the philosophy of the Bantus, and first try to understand it from their point of view. I ask you to read this study without prejudice, and without Thomism, as something new'.[65] Beyond this, his central argument is that the route of 'putting in contact' is the royal one that will let the evangelical message find its way into Bantu hearts and lead to conversion: and this is because the message itself will have found, beneath the static language of being–substance, its original force as a vitalism. Tempels writes:

> I believe precisely that the Primitives will receive, from the best among Occidentals, the most beautiful thing that man can receive: the plenitude of the Good News, the Christ, the Giver of Life, of this full life that the Bantu's hearts have yearned towards for centuries; but I also believe that, on the other hand, the Primitives will give us a precious gift in exchange: the knowledge of ourselves, the return to the original, healthier, and more natural foundations of ourselves and of what is authentically human.... We – and all Occidentals – must return to original nature, this jewel that God has not destroyed but has rather rendered supernatural.[66]

Placide Tempels here speaks of 'Primitives' rather than of 'Bantu' and in his correspondence, he generalizes his fundamental thesis more and more to the point that it becomes 'the conception that all non-Christian humanity (Chinese, Hindu, Primitive) has of the internal dynamism of being, the internal forces of growth, reduction of being, influence of being, the vital hierarchy', while admitting that this amounted to a '"thinking" that does not entirely agree with scholasticism (your great scandal! [this is directed to Fr. Hulstaert – author's note]) but which is not irreconcilable with the healthy "thinking" of a normally thinking man'.[67] Tempels' letter to Hulstaert, dated 10 December 1946, from which this quotation is drawn, is an essential text for anyone today who wants to understand what Tempels' project was, beyond its contradictory aspects. That he claimed to be 'happy' to see his correspondent agreeing that he had 'described things that are not specifically Bantu or primitive but universally human' is accordingly very important, as is the way in which, in concluding, he sees the ultimate significance of his work:

> I am pursuing the construction of the foundations of Christian (Chinese, Hindu, and Primitive) philosophy, and it will flourish; otherwise Christ will not be born in the soul of the Primitives. In addition, I believe we must submit the conceptually petrified

souls of Europe to a rejuvenating cure; this will be the retribution, on the part of the Primitives, for the sweat and blood the Europeans have shed for them.[68]

We see, then, that the philosophical object defined in the seven theses and named *Bantu Philosophy* has ended up freeing itself from its specific and exclusive incarnation in the Bantus' view of the world in order to become a sort of *universal monadology* where a truly *first* philosophy expresses itself, where being–force is not yet frozen into substance. The effort of translating it from a language where it gives itself to be read immediately into a language becomes, in Europe, that of philosophy; ultimately signifies the task of guiding this latter back towards a retrieved childhood where it (re)discovers itself as a philosophy of life (and therefore, according to Tempels, a Christian one).[69] What Bergson might call the Belgian missionary's primary intuition, ultimately, is that the Bantu *speak* a philosophy of life which therefore is theirs, and equally Africa's, but which is also, more generally, 'universally human'. Beneath the evident and inevitable colonial paternalism there is also a man of the church's homage to those who, in his eyes, were no longer simply pagans. Thanks to them, he had understood that the Message whose servant he was, in expressing itself historically as theology in the language of a philosophy that spoke a self-declared 'historical' language, had cast itself into a static ontology, that of the attribution of predicates to a being–substance. Being, always overflowing itself, the superabundant life that is the original sense of the Message, had found itself, so to speak, compromised and constricted in an overly immobile language. Tempels tells the story of his discovery (could we say his conversion?), thanks to the other's revealing itself as the same, of that which is situated beyond being, is 'otherwise than being', which is life.

The non-Aristotelianism of Alexis Kagamé, for its part, is expressed in this priest's project of excavating, out of the grammar of the Bantu languages in which it is incarnated, the linguistic-philosophy they carry in a manner analogous to the way that Aristotelian *onto-logy* is entirely inscribed in Greek grammar, and perhaps in other languages of the same family. So Kagamé established, beginning from the Kinyarwanda language, a table of four categories that responds, to some extent, to Aristotle's table of nine or ten categories.[70]

On the question of the relation between 'categories of language' and 'categories of thought', to adapt the title of the article by Benvéniste, we can usefully consult this often-quoted philological remark of Nietzsche's:

> The strange family resemblance of all Indian, Greek, and German philosophizing speaks for itself clearly enough. Where there are linguistic affinities, then because of the common philosophy of grammar (I mean: due to the unconscious domination and direction through similar grammatical functions), it is obvious that everything lies ready from the very start for a similar development and sequence of philosophical systems; on the other hand, the way seems as good as blocked for certain other possibilities of interpreting the world. Philosophers of the Ural-Altaic language group (where the concept of the subject is the most poorly developed) are more likely to 'see the world' differently, and to be found on paths different from those taken by the Indo-Germans or Muslims: the spell of particular grammatical functions is in the last analysis the spell of *physiological* value judgements and racial conditioning. – So much towards a rejection of Locke's superficiality with regard to the origin of ideas.[71]

For Kagamé, the philosophy he calls 'Euro-American' needs to be set side-by-side with a Bantu philosophy where, in particular, 'the verb *to be* only serves the role of *copula* and consequently must be accompanied by an attribute or a circumstantial complement referring to place'. Consequently, he adds, 'The famous formula, *I think, therefore I am*, has absolutely no meaning in Bantu languages'.[72]

The question that should be posed to this last statement is this: if *I think, therefore I am* has no sense in Bantu languages, then what about its Kinyarwanda translation? It is true that for certain languages the verb 'to be' has no role other than that of copula. Wolof, which

I speak, is one of these languages. But it nonetheless remains that Wolof, like any other language, Bantu or not, has the resources to translate the *Discourse on Method* and the formula of the cogito at its heart.

To better understand the importance of this question of translation, compare Kagamé's exclusively relativistic position (there are different philosophical grammars, and therefore languages with cogito and languages without cogito) to the path taken by the Ghanaian philosopher Kwasi Wiredu in his reflection 'The concept of truth in Akan language'. Wiredu explains that, to the extent that 'truth' is taken in a purely cognitive sense (rather than in the moral sense of veridicity), there is no Akan word for this concept, a situation not without analogy to the one Kagamé found concerning the words *to be*. But he does this in order to show that this fact allows philosophical questions connected to the notion of truth, for example the theory of truth as correspondence between a statement and reality, to be put to the test of *translation*. 'These linguistic contrasts [between Akan and English]', he writes, 'have some very interesting consequences for the theory of truth'.[73]

Generally speaking, this back-and-forth between English and Akan, the path of translation, that is to say of putting in touch, allows the Ghanaian philosopher to conduct an important reflection on the fact that questions have a way of becoming in some way clarified once they are posed simultaneously in English and in Akan. This leads to the investigation of what a philosophical problem is and what it means for a question to be universally posed:

> Now, although it is, I think, correct to say that a problem like the one about the relation between truth and fact arises out of the nature of the vocabulary of English, it does not follow that it is not a genuine philosophical issue in English. The concepts of truth and fact are among the most fundamental concepts of human thought. Without the notion of something being a fact or of a proposition being true thinking is inconceivable unless it be a mere succession of ideas, and even that can be doubted. It seems obvious, then, that the relation between the

terms 'truth' and 'fact' is a philosophical issue; for, of course, one cannot give a fundamental clarification of any of these foundational concepts in English without relating them one to the other. Yet, since these terms need not be both present in all natural languages, as the case of Akan shows, this task is not inescapable for the human mind. From which it follows that some philosophical problems are not universal.[74]

The majority of African philosophers believe the moment has come to philosophize in African languages. This task can be thought of as the will to produce an *other* philosophy, which would keep close to each language's ways of speaking: this is Kagamé's route. It can also be thought of as a means of thinking philosophically in translation and in crossing perspectives: this is the route than an analysis such as 'The concept of truth in Akan language' opens up. There is every reason to believe this is the route of the future.

Proof by Aesthetics

In his book *The Mind of Africa*, speaking of the Akan people, W.E. Abraham wrote:

> As the Akans could not write, they expressed their philosophico-religious ideas through art, through the timeless, immemorial, silent, and elemental power so characteristic of African traditional art. Indeed this is the main reason why it was not life-like in a representational sense. Forms had to be distorted. In art, there was a moral-philosophical preoccupation which led it to portray forces of the world, and to portray a force it was essential that it should not be treated like something assimilated, and consequently like something overcome, as the rendering of it in life-like figures would have been.[75]

Against 'critics like Gombrich' (the art historian Ernst Gombrich) who argue that African artists were simply incapable of realistic representation, Abraham claims that an artist was perfectly capable, when the goal was realistic reproduction, of providing representations that resembled their model: for example, figurines of Nigerian chiefs were produced for archival purposes. But this is not the goal pursued by 'moral art, the art whose inspiration is the intuition of a world force'.[76]

Abraham's reflection on the generally non-realistic forms of what has been called 'negro art' could be taken as expressing the idea that African aesthetics would be the living manifestation of the philosophical object, defined in the seven theses which Tempels saw as 'Bantu philosophy'.[77] African art would then be a 'proof' of the Belgian missionary's hypothesis or, as Léo Apostel would say, the writing, in an alphabet of forms, of the philosophy of forces. This art would then be *first* art in the sense that the philosophy which it translates into its language is *first philosophy*.[78]

That the arts of Africa are the language and, as it were, the writing of the philosophy of forces is also precisely the thesis that Senghor upheld, beginning with his first philosophical writings.[79] If, in contrast to his friend Césaire, Senghor did not dwell on the motivations of colonial (or neocolonial) 'governmentality' behind Tempels' project of exposing Bantu philosophy, this was because his own reflections found a particular echo in the missionary's book. These reflections especially concerned African art considered as expression of the force of life. This, at least, was what Senghor tried to say in one of his very first essays, 'What the black man contributes' ('Ce que l'homme noir apporte'), published in 1939. In this essay drawing on his readings on negro art, the Senegalese poet explored the concept of 'rhythm' which, he claimed following the work of Paul Guillaume and Thomas Munro he had read carefully,[80] characterized what was then called 'negro style'. Where Abraham would later speak of a 'moral art' opposed to the ideal of resemblance, Senghor in his 1939 essay spoke of a *spiritual art* which aimed at 'the *essential* expression of the object' and which is therefore 'opposed to *subjective realism*'.[81] To refute the idea that non-realism is the sign of an inability, he wrote: 'Where many have wanted to see nothing but the clumsiness of hands or an incapacity to observe reality, there is a *will*, at the very least the consciousness of an ordination, or better: a subordination'.[82]

'Subordination', then, to the force which commands, and which is rhythm:

> This ordering force that constitutes negro style is *rhythm*. It is the most sensible and the least material thing. It is the vital element par excellence. It is the primary condition for, and the sign of art, as respiration is of life; respiration that rushes or slows down, becomes regular or spasmodic, depending on the being's tension, the degree and quality of the emotion. Such is rhythm, originally, in its purity, such is it in the masterpieces of negro art, particularly in sculpture. It is composed of one theme – sculptural form – that is opposed to a brother theme, like inhalation is opposed to exhalation, and that is reprised again. It is not a symmetry that engenders monotony; rhythm is alive, it is free. For reprise is not redundancy, or repetition. The theme is reprised at another place, on another level, in another combination, in a variation; and it produces something like another tone, another timbre, another accent. And the general effect is intensified by this, not without nuances. This is how rhythm acts, despotically, on what is least intellectual in us, to make us enter into the *spirituality of the object*; and this attitude of abandon that we have is itself rhythmic.[83]

We can see that the vitalist language of Senghorian aesthetics can only find itself in deep accord with the philosophy of living force that Tempels described as Bantu. Senghor returned to the notion of rhythm in an article on 'Negro-African aesthetics' published in 1956 in the journal *Diogène*:

> *What is rhythm?* It is the architecture of being, the internal dynamism that gives it form, the system of waves it emanates towards the *Others*, the pure expression of vital Force. Rhythm is the vibrating shock, the force that, through the senses, seizes us as the root of being. It expresses itself through the most material and sensual means: lines, surfaces, colours, and volumes, in architecture, sculpture and painting; accents in poetry and music; movement in dance. But, in doing so, it

organizes all this concreteness toward the light of the *Spirit*. For the Negro African, it is in so far as it is incarnate in sensuality that rhythm illuminates the spirit.[84]

Senghorian aesthetics make force, above all, a rhythm. The ontology of forces here becomes more precisely one of rhythm, and artistic creation is the art of combining rhythms, or rhythmic series. For Senghor, at root, if aesthetics verify and confirm *Bantu philosophy* it is because the latter *is*, in itself, an aesthetics, and accordingly we can add the following corollaries to its constitutive theses:

C1: What defines the individuality of a force it its rhythm.

C2: One opens up to the object by a *rhythmic attitude* that comes into phase with it. This attitude is constitutive of aesthetic emotion.

C3: A force-rhythm in the work of art harmoniously arranges the different rhythms that constitute it and combines them into an organic whole.[85]

So, to conclude, what should we think of the thesis that African art, in its dominant traits that reoccur across different cultural regions of the continent, is the proof of a philosophy of the force of life?

First of all, it should not mean that the existence of an 'ethnic' philosophy has been proven, one that would be a worldview carried and shared by the whole group, whether a linguistic group such as the Bantu or, more broadly, of Africans 'in general'. The critique of ethno-philosophy is correct: an ethnic worldview carried by every element of the group and naturally expressed in its language, gestures, judgements, postures, et cetera, and serving as thought, makes very little sense.

This thesis, then, needs to be examined by beginning with the work of art itself, in the way it presents itself as a language of forms. This requires bracketing the circumstances of its creation, and in particular the religious ones: we will be considering it starting from what Malraux would call its 'metamorphosis', once it has ceased to be the receptacle of the divine that it might have been in the eyes of those who produced it. We will treat it as if it is born under the gaze that gives it life, careful not to pin it like a dead butterfly upon a card together with the inventory of ethnographic details which certainly provide its history, but which can hardly explain its *presence*: its existence outside of its own time and, since it no more belongs to the one in which it is regarded, outside of time.

This thesis would mean that the way the object speaks compellingly gestures towards the language of the life force, the force-rhythm that Senghor explores, and that it need not be specific to Africa for it to give an explanation of the way in which this continent's art at large turns its back on mimetic representation to bring a world of forces to light.

The Time we Need

*Our civilization can hardly detach itself from its fascination
with the past. It can only dream of the future, and when it
does elaborate projects that are more than simple dreams, it
draws them on a canvas where once again the past projects
itself. It is retrospective, and stubbornly so.*

Gaston Berger[86]

When the philosopher Gaston Berger (1896–1960) suggests that in
the mobile world where we live, which is not only changing but
changing more and more rapidly according to an 'immediately
perceptible acceleration' that 'affects us directly',[87] it is necessary 'to
develop prospective disciplines' (in particular a 'prospective
anthropology'), and to develop a 'prospective attitude' in general,[88]
who is he addressing?[89] Which 'us' does he invite to tear ourselves
away from a certain 'retrospective stubbornness' to which our
'fascination with the past' tends to confine us? A reader would initially
consider this to refer to humanity in general, the one that philosophers
speak of when they say 'us' and even when they say 'I'. But after this
first response, readers might ask themselves if 'our civilization', from
Berger's pen, is in fact simply human civilization or, on the contrary,
what Western civilization is called. This is because some might think
to set opposite to this 'prospective anthropology' (which takes it
upon itself, for example, to show 'what aspects of mankind's situation

in tomorrow's world it is possible to perceive today', or 'to determine in what sense and to what extent the profound transformation of situations influences the posing and perhaps the solution of traditional philosophical problems')[90] an anthropology of cultures separated by the different conceptions (or even formulations) that they have of this or that 'philosophical problem' – and, in particular, of the problem of time, the meaning given to the past, present and future.

Should it be taken as a fact that cultures differ in that they are characterized by different conceptions of time? In particular, should the notion of an 'African conception of time', which is often evoked in ethnological discourse and which Africans are not necessarily the last to apply to themselves, be accorded meaning? In February 2007, a speech given by the President of the French Republic, Nicolas Sarkozy, at the University of Dakar presented as a fact the idea that Africans have their own conception of time, which explains why they have 'insufficiently entered into History'. This revival of the cliché in which a particular sense of time prevents African peoples from synchronizing with the rhythm of an accelerating world provoked, understandably, astonishment and shock: the mere posture of the French President administering to his African interlocutors a lesson in the psychology of peoples so as to explain their own condition to them, under the pretext of 'straight talk', was the height of incongruity.[91] But, this said, it must be noted that the way in which this speech recycled old ethnological chestnuts was not really in discord with the general climate of what has been called *Afropessimism*, a discourse that offers, with various inflections, the desperate and despairing idea that Africa's problem, ultimately, is Africa itself.

Afropessimism rests on the proposition that the reasons for the continent's 'lagging' behind the rest of the world can be found in the culture, in the worldview of Africans, since, it is claimed, as all the different economic recipes have proved ineffective, there is something in Africanity which constitutes, ultimately, a genuine 'refusal' of development.[92] Nothing better expresses the quintessence of Afropessimism, this idea that Africa is a separate case – a 'basket case' – than those lines with which Jean Bonvin, the then president of the OECD's Centre for Development, introduced a work his institution published, titled *Whither African Economies?*[93]

> For OECD Member countries, doing everything they can to help Africa fill the gap – which in the past 30 years has grown wider – is both a human obligation and an absolute necessity.

> For economists, it is also an intellectual challenge. While for some 20 years success has followed upon success in East Asia and then in Latin America, we seem to be incapable of coming up with solutions that are appropriate for Africa – despite a mass of research, economic-policy recommendations of all kinds and considerable financial and technological assistance.[94]

Africa, then, is an intellectual challenge for economists: one could hardly express better the idea that, ultimately, nothing works on this special continent, where some even saw in the last of the twentieth century's genocides, the indescribable horror of Rwanda in 1994, just yet another African tragedy.

If, then, the *ultima ratio* of African backwardness is to be found in culture, at the heart of this is time. In response to the indignant and mocking reactions to President Sarkozy's 'Dakar discourse', the advisor who prepared his text for him tried to call the thought of Senghor to his defence, claiming that they agreed in their understanding of the African worldview. Senghor, for whom prospective was a major theme, would certainly not provide him material to support his 'thesis'.[95] On the other hand, he might have invoked what John Mbiti wrote with regard to an African conception of time, in his work on 'African religions and philosophy'.[96]

That Time we call African

At the heart of the question of there being a cultural dimension to development, John Mbiti poses that of time. From the conception Africans have of time, he declares, flows their attitudes, beliefs and practices, and their philosophy of the future in particular. He expresses this in seven principle theses:

1. *Time is composed of events.* What this first thesis, or rather definition, tells us is that time cannot be understood to be other than what happens. Not what happens *in* it, or what is produced *inside it;* because it would be inconceivable that time would continue to exist after all the events it is considered to contain have been extracted from it, in some sort of thought experiment. In the same way that, Mbiti says, 'it is the content which defines space',[97] it is the event which defines time. We could say that time is *the fullness* of events. It is neither their frame in a Kantian sense, nor the order of their succession in a Leibnizian sense: it simply is not without them. Time is the event, it is not outside of it in the way the container remains exterior to its contents.

2. *The past is the most important dimension of time.* We see immediately how this thesis follows from the preceding one. If time is the fullness of events then it only *is* if, in essence, it is what has already come. It identifies completely with the past, which is nothing but the events that *have taken place.*

3. *The present is continually in motion towards the past.* Once again, this thesis is a consequence of the first. It means that, to evoke an image of flux that always seems to present itself naturally, the river of time flows upstream, from the present towards the past. This is on the physical level; on the metaphysical level, it means that the present takes its meaning from the past towards which it is oriented. To evoke a maritime image this time, which might also be that of an endless hourglass, the *now* of our conscience and of our actions is called forth and snatched by the ocean of past events which receives, over and over, indefinitely, like drops that fall without ever adding anything to it, those events that we call our present.

4. *There is virtually no future.* This thesis, once again, is a necessary conclusion from the definition of time, because to think of a future event entails a veritable contradiction. John Mbiti writes accordingly that 'time is a two-dimensional phenom-

enon, with a long *past*, a *present* and virtually *no future*.'[98] The only 'stub' of a future that we can say exists is one that retro-projects itself, so to say, into the present, as a trace-announce-ment. It is made up of what we could call *quasi-events*, in the sense that the present is already pregnant with them, and that they can already be read, now, in the same way that the har-vest announces itself in the promise of the flowers or the child in the swelling belly of the mother. It is not by chance that the examples that come to mind, like these, express the idea of an *organic* link between what is now and what will come. In prac-tice, this means that a future cannot be imagined beyond the horizon of a few months, beyond tomorrow, beyond the shadow that it projects behind itself, already, in the now.

5. *African languages and calendars manifest and prove these theses.* The best witness to an African conception of time comes, it seems, from the way in which time is expressed in languages and whose unfolding can be read in calendars. In fact, John Mbiti presents his analysis of the East African languages in which he conducted his research as a 'test' for 'his findings'. Examining verbal tenses in the Kikamba and Kikuyu languages in particular, he believes he can confirm in conclusion 'that there are no concrete words or expressions to convey the idea of a distant future',[99] one that would stretch out in front of us beyond the horizon of a few months, or two years at most. He then presents what he calls 'phenomenon calendars', as opposed to purely mathematical numerical calendars which, he explains, are not linked to real phenomena that are produced while producing time. In a manner similar to how clock time differs from the time that measures an activity, in these phenomenon calendar hours and months (lunar months, of course) are given names that refer to particular periodic events: for instance, 'leading out the herd' in the morning and the evening, or 'the heat of the sun', a phenomenon that gave its name to the month that corresponds to October in the language of the Latuka people.[100]

6. *Long-term planning is foreign to society.* This is one of the crucial consequences of John Mbiti's theses, above all in light of the need that African societies have today of developing prospective capacity. The Kenyan philosopher writes: 'So African peoples have no belief in progress', the idea that the course of human activities and achievements moves from a low to a higher degree. 'The people neither plan for the distant future nor "build castles in the air". The centre of gravity of human thought and action lies in the past', writes Mbiti.[101] And he insists that the many ethnologically-derived declarations about a properly African manner of *wasting* time should be taken as evidence of a specific philosophy of time. Once what time signifies for Africans is fully understood, attitudes taken to be an art of wasting time appear more clearly as those of 'either waiting for time or in the process of "producing" time'.[102]

7. *The futural dimension of time was imposed on Africans from outside and they have still not fully appropriated it.* In other terms, it took a catastrophe, in the sense of a brutal rupture in the course of things, for African societies to discover or to extend the futural dimension of time. This catastrophe presented itself in the form of 'Christian missionary teaching', or in the garb of a Western-type education or of modern technology. It has led to 'national planning for economic growth, political independence, extension of educational facilities and so on'.[103] And because it involved a rupture, the process could not have avoided being a bumpy one. Here is what, according to Mbiti, is 'at the root of ... the political instability of our nations'. Africa therefore naturally finds itself in a structural crisis which, in philosophical terms, translates the catastrophe caused by the eruption of the future into a worldview where the past is everything, memory is the essence, and tradition is the source of meaning.

John Mbiti concludes his chapter on 'the concept of time' by inviting the criticism, which he understands to be inevitable, to proceed in what he thinks will be most the productive manner. He asks those who will reject his theses, most likely seeing them, he says, as a continuation of Lévy-Bruhl's writings on prelogical mentality,[104] to take the time to propose 'another sustained analysis of African concepts of time' rather than simply saying 'yes' or 'no' to his own conclusions. The burden of proof, he believes, is on his opponents who will need to find counter-examples to weaken what he has put forward.

Words to Speak of Time

In throwing out this challenge, the Kenyan philosopher has in mind an eventual counter-argument that would take the same form as the proof he provided for his theses: one based in linguistic analysis and in examining ways of speaking of time. Therefore, a critical analysis of the concept of time, according to John Mbiti, must start with that of his fifth thesis.

Carrying out such an examination should begin by observing that, in the end, it is not very helpful to proceed as the Kenyan philosopher invites us to do and to seek out other ways of speaking of time in other African languages from other regions, as Kwame Gyekye did when he sought to counter Mibiti's theses by demonstrating the conception of time according to the Akan people.[105] In the end all this provides is a simple back-and-forth between an example here and a counter-example there, ultimately bringing thesis and antithesis back-to-back. In reality, it is the very idea of a proof by language that turns out to be pure sophism because, as we have already said, it is entirely reliant on a method of over-analysing African languages as 'concrete' and, on the other hand, seeing only abstract significations in European languages. To recall: the names in the 'Western' calendar, *juin* or *June*, *août* or *August*, *mars* or *March*, are no more or less 'concrete' in themselves than those of the 'African' calendar that Mbiti studies. Similarly, take the time to ask yourself about the etymology of well-known measures of time like the hour, the minute or the second, and you will see that the adoption of these terms to indicate the 24th of a day, the 60th or the 360th part of an hour, respectively, involves quite a history.

Calendars and temporal divisions may have their *origins* in certain phenomena, but these more or less disappear afterwards, behind their numerical *usage*.

Let us recall, as Barbara Cassin continues to invite us to do, that before these were concepts they were words that we speak and write. What is understood by the word '*avenir*' ('future') itself, the one that Mbiti says expresses in French a dimension that does not exist in the Kikamba and the Kikuyu languages on which he bases his analyses? This word can always be seen as concrete, indicating what is 'to come'.[106] In how long? In what horizon? Nothing in the word itself indicates this. It may be an immediate future, one already announced in the present, or a more distant temporal horizon: the future lasts a more or less long time. Consider the following phrase in Wolof, the most commonly spoken language in Senegal: *ligeey ngir ëllëg*. It means, literally, *to work for tomorrow*. Why does 'tomorrow' here need to mean, precisely and concretely, the day coming after the one where we are, or, at most, in two years, while the same usage of 'tomorrow' to refer to the future in English is required to summon up the image of a line drawing itself indefinitely into the future? This makes no sense, of course, since the words *ëllëg* in Wolof, *demain* in French or *tomorrow* in English can all be adapted to the same functions when it comes to evoking the future.

Ultimately, John Mbiti himself should be invited to make a further examination of the words used in language, and particularly of the ones, *Sasa* and *Zamani*, whose use he proposes in order to avoid the representations which would irresistibly be evoked by the English words *past, present* and *future*. *Sasa* and *Zamani*, Mbiti says, are Swahili words, *Sasa* covering the 'now-period', from a future restricted to what is about to arrive up to the recent past, while *Zamani* is the past without limit. *Sasa*, the Kenyan philosopher tells us, is continually swallowed by *Zamani*, into which it disappears. And from the concept of time he draws that of oral history, and declares that no eschatology can exist here:

> If we attempt to fit such traditions into a mathematical time-scale, they would appear to cover only a few centuries whereas

in reality they stretch much further back; and some of them, being in the form of myths, defy any attempt to describe them on a mathematical time-scale. In any case, oral history has no dates to be remembered. Man looks back from whence he came, and man is certain that nothing will bring this world to a conclusion. According to this interpretation of African view of history, there are innumerable myths about Zamani, but no myths about any end of the world, since time has no end. African peoples expect human history to continue forever, in the rhythm of moving from the Sasa to the Zamani and there is nothing to suggest that this rhythm shall ever come to an end: the days, months, seasons and years have no end, just as there is no end to the rhythm of birth, marriage, procreation and death.[107]

One should be aware that *Sasa* and *Zamani* are certainly Swahili words, but they *also* have an Arabic origin. This fact is important, and it is baffling that Mbiti hardly considers its implications while he claims to be basing his examination on the very words that make up language. Generally speaking, the hybridization between the Arabic language and the other languages of the continent (Swahili being without doubt the language where this hybridization is most pronounced) is a phenomenon which ought to be given full consideration in an examination of philosophical questions in the African context. We can note then here that the word 'zamân' (2E'F) signifies in Arabic 'epoch', 'era', 'period', 'time'; while the word 'sâ'a' (3'9)), which is doubled in 'sasa', signifies 'the moment', 'the instant', 'the time'.

Undoubtedly, it would be interesting to ask why, in their process of hybridization with Arabic, other African languages came almost systematically to adopt Arabic words for speaking of time. We can compare the Swahili words for time with those of a language from extreme West Africa like Senegambian Wolof, where we also say *jamano* (derived from *zamân*) for period, era, time, and *saa* for an instant (*ci saasi*, for example, means 'this instant', 'immediately') while the doubled form '*saa i saa*' means 'at certain moments', 'from time to time'.

These sorts of considerations about hybridization and the comparisons that it calls for put John Mbiti's essentialist conclusions into question, along with the insistence on the concrete character of African languages that he invokes in support of his thesis: no word is in itself the proof of an African conception of time for which only the concrete past and present exist, and of which it would be the natural expression. And the thesis that the future dimension of time came to Africans from outside provokes this simple question: if the Arabic *zamân*, which became the Swahili *zamani*, carries for its part a futural and eschatological dimension (the Arabic expression *âkhiru zamân* means 'the end of time'), then how did this dimension subsequently come to disappear in the *usage* of this word by the populations Mbiti considers – particularly given that this dimension is present in the same word adapted into different contexts, for instance in *jamano*? Would it not be better to simply conclude that, in the end, words have no natural concrete sense, but rather have usages? And that these usages themselves depend on the history of the societies being considered? Accordingly, Muslim African societies where the idea of time marching to its end provides a religious, metaphysical dimension would have maintained, in various forms of the word, the futural dimension that *zamân* can contain.

To Foresee or to Anticipate

The Cameroonian philosopher Engelbert Mveng (1930–95) insisted on the need to distinguish between a 'concept of time' that is, he writes 'a mental perception … abstract, objective, and universal' and a 'conception of time' inscribed in culture.[108] Accordingly, there would be 'as many conceptions of time as there are types of civilization'. Above all, his reflection intends to show that beyond the differences whose marks can be seen in languages, the question of time determines the human condition in general. Father Mveng sees an expression of African wisdom in a myth 'that tells how men, terrified by Death, went to find their Lord God to say to him: "Take the specter of Death away from us!" God looked them in their eyes and said: "Go and teach your children that from now on, without Death, Life would no longer be Life!" So the men understood that they must defeat Death to attain to true Life'.[109] Clearly, like many myths, this one easily comes away from its source as told by 'African wisdom' to express the simply universal human truth that that our experience of time comes essentially from the fact that we know we will be given over to death, and that as a result it is our duty to defeat it by bringing life into being, the true one that is out of its reach.

So, in the struggle that 'opposes Life and Death in us ... each instant is therefore always new, at once the seed of the future and the totality of a project'. Engelbert Mveng here cites a saying from the 'sorcerer of [his] village' who said: 'man always makes the time he needs'. Let us pause on this saying that, for the Cameroonian philosopher, meant that time is the 'infinite deployment of our being'.[110] Our capacity to create time by means of our project has nothing to do, anymore, with a cultural conception expressed in the calendar used in the sorcerer's village, or in the verbal tenses of the languages spoken there. We do not need to find out if the future is *given* in these languages as the time of a sufficiently far-off future: we assert that the future is what we *create*. Contrary to John Mbiti's approach, this means that human languages will not allow us to read in them a division of cultures into those where a prospective vision exists and those where it does not. Such an approach assumes that language names what can be seen and that what can be seen is only what language names: the language that says 'future' and 'prospective' is inscribed within a culture that *sees* far into the future and in which, therefore, a genuine prospective sense has developed. But to speak this way is to miss the simple fact that the future is not something to be *seen*. John Mbiti's point is valid, but not in the sense he believes. If it is true that time is, in fact, made up of what happens, and consequently does not extend itself as if into a void in the direction of the future, then this truth is not only the truth of a particular human culture but is *ours*, all of us, humanity as such. John Mbiti does not express the truth of a Bantu or African conception of time;

he rediscovers a universal, human truth, one that is at the heart of the thought of Henri Bergson, for whom time is duration.

Gaston Berger tells a story about 'a Negro king':

> An explorer of the last century arrives at the court of a Negro king, who puts the White's spectacles on his nose. By chance, they correct his congenital myopia. Upon seeing distances that he had never dreamed of, the king's enthusiasm was such that he gave the explorer every possible assistance ... in exchange for his pair of glasses.[111]

From this story, the 'father of prospective' draws the following lesson:

> Congenitally myopic with regard to the vision of the future, we are beginning to think that there are distances there to see, that we can see, and that we must bring ourselves to see.[112]

The story Berger tells might seem to correspond with John Mbiti's propositions. According to him, foreign culture and language, naturally laden with the future and prospective, come to be superimposed on the traditional 'vision' of 'indigenous' culture and language, which discover that they are 'myopic' after this contact. The new language then allows for seeing better, and seeing further, which is to say seeing deeper into the future that from then on will exist for eyes that are now equipped, for the first time, with the spectacles they unknowingly needed. At its base, rather than a story about a 'Negro king', Berger could just as easily have evoked the history of modern science and the invention of the telescope that allowed Galileo to *see* what no human eye had seen before, in the process upturning the edifice of the Aristotelian and Ptolemaic world.

Berger also poses the question of a language that can speak of the future in reference to the Biblical story of Isaiah, who had a vision of what was to come but encountered the limits of language when he tried to communicate its reality to his people. 'Isaiah', he writes, 'who did not have available, in Hebrew, a verbal form expressing the future, tried (with some vehemence) to show what the others did not see, could not see, refused to see: that the future is there, close by, the future that will come upon those who are stubbornly blind, incapable of opening their eyes. He tries, he insists, he repeats, like a schoolmaster with sullen children, with demonstrations and images, warning and threatening'.[113]

What is said here of Hebrew applies to the languages John Mbiti examines: the future, properly speaking, does not exist. So the prophet finds himself invested in the impossible mission of *telling* a future that he can see but which, literally, does not *speak* to his people. But let us ask what the prophet Isaiah really *wants* to do with his vision. Does he mean to bring the people to devote themselves, miraculously, to seeing beyond the present, that is to say: beyond their language? Such a demand for the democratization of the capacity to prophesy (which is not the same thing as the prophetic faculty which might be, for its part, a component of our common humanity) would be senseless. What the prophets want, when they grow impatient and exasperated, irritated and exhausted, is *action*, in the present, in accordance with what the future demands. Or better: action with the aim of bringing such a future into being. And so, as Berger wrote of what can be learned from Henri Bergson, the philosopher of whom it is rightly said that he 'opened' our conception of time: 'the future is no longer what inevitably must be produced, it is not even what will happen; it is what the world as a whole will make'.[114]

Berger's examples, then, contrary to what a first reading might suggest, lead us in the end to the opposite of John Mbiti's theses. For all the Bergsonian philosophy of prospective is there to remind us of this: prospective is not a matter of *seeing* in order to then *say* what we see; it is engagement in *action*. It is a matter, Berger says, of passing from 'seeing' to 'acting'. In other words, underneath the language of fore-seeing one should hear the prospective *attitude*, the *disposition* towards anticipation. That we must therefore create the time that we need is something that no culture or language, coming from outside, will teach.

Speech and Ink

The Word, said Ogotemmêli, is for everyone in this world; it must come and go and be interchanged, for it is good to give and to receive the forces of life.[115]

The West African thinker Amadou Hampâté Bâ (1900–91) is often cited as having said 'In Africa, an elder who dies is a library in flames'.[116] This statement is so celebrated that it has gained the status of a proverb, in the sense that no one quite knows any more if it has a precise author. If this has occurred, it is because this statement perfectly expresses different elements that come to mind when one thinks of orality. First of all, there is the idea that orality is a fundamental characteristic of African cultures and even constitutes their spirit; then there is the idea that to think of orality is always to think in terms of the question of its transmission; and then, finally, there is the sense of an urgency today, linked precisely to this question of transmission: that orality is fragile like the memory of the ancestors; that the continuity of its passage is menaced by rupture, synonymous with death; that it must be preserved at all cost and that the inevitable disappearance of elders must not mean the destruction of the African library in the flames of forgetfulness.

Each of these three aspects poses a set of questions for examination.

Sense of Urgency and the Passage to Writing

The sense of an urgent need to archive quickly, in a race with death, is also an anguish born from sensing the fragility of things, of memory first of all, but also of culture in general. In this spirit Amadou Hampâté Bâ assigned himself the task of being a traditionist, a transcriber and translator into French of West African oral literature. From the late 1930s, when he took the initiative of contacting Théodore Monod (who would bring him shortly thereafter to IFAN,[117] which he directed) to ask for assistance in making the works of wisdom and beauty of Fulfulde culture known in French, and up until the publication of his memoirs, he himself was steadily becoming an elder; one who, for posterity, had transcribed into books and stored in the library what was living – and barely surviving – in orality.

Texts in defence and illustration of a 'Negro literature' existing in the oral repertoire, or 'orature' as it is also called, were not something new. For instance, the Abbot Grégoire wrote a book with the title *De la littérature des Nègres* (On Negro literature). We find there, to cite just one example, the idea that what passes for literary and artistic creation in Europe always has its *equivalent* in African orature: 'France had formerly her Trouveres and Troubadours', Abbot Grégoire wrote, 'and Scotland, her Minstrels. Negroes have theirs, named Griots, who attend kings, and like the others, praise and lie with wit'.[118]

The poet Blaise Cendrars evoked a similar principle of equivalence. At the end of the brief introductory 'notice' to his *Anthologie Nègre*, a collection of various myths, tales and stories that he published in order to demonstrate the 'beauty' and the 'plastic capacity of the languages' and oral literatures of Africa, he said that there was now proof of the 'law of intellectual constancy glimpsed by Rémy de Groumont',[119] according to which the human spirit (and its production) was everywhere identical, in opposition to Lévy-Bruhlien ethnology which was dedicated to inventing different humanities.

Let's return to Amadou Hampâté Bâ. In an interview he gave during the 1970s, he spoke of his religiously-inspired poems written in Peul as his only 'creative works'.[120] By this he suggested that in this language he had been able to participate in literature as creative activity, while in French he had only made an act of transcribing or translating. Birago Diop, another 'transciber' of orature, also expressed this opinion when he claimed to be only the translator of Amadou Koumba, whose name appears beside his, as a kind of co-author, on the cover of *Contes d'Amadou Koumba* and of *Nouveaux contes d'Amadou Koumba*. But Léopold Sédar Senghor warns us not to be fooled by these coquetries. 'Birago Diop', he wrote (and this would certainly apply to others, the Ivoirian Bernard Dadié for example, and also Hampâté Bâ, however much of a 'traditionist' he might have claimed to be), 'is not satisfied by word for word. He has lived … the griot's stories; he has, as an artist who is Black and French at the same time, rethought and written them, remembering that "traduttore traditore"'.[121]

Senghor is right, when discussing the passage from orature to writing, to invite us to reflect on the meaning of transcription/translation. Is translation treason? Certainly: Birago Diop scrupulously declared that the flavour of the texts he writes is nothing compared to what the 'the voice, verve and expression' of his 'old griot' produces.[122] Undoubtedly, this regret should be understood as expressing the 'work of mourning' that, according to Paul Ricoeur, the translator always performs, since in carrying out the task with which she is charged, she becomes aware that it is possible only on the condition of 'some acceptance of loss'.[123] In effect, he explains, evoking Freud, 'the work of remembering' taken on by translation is one side of the coin whose other is 'the work of mourning'. This thesis can be applied, with remarkable results, to the question of 'rescuing' orature by means of the passage into writing, by transcription.

Translation is treason? Certainly, but this betrayal is the only true fidelity. In the same way that there is no perfect translation against which we could measure the gap between what is and what could have been,[124] there is little reason to treat the written text as the shadow of the 'true' text that it would be 'orally', as it might have been *spoken* by Amadou Koumba. There is something paradoxical in the claim that orality must be quickly transcribed and archived before it dies with the elders. To say this is to admit that it is at any rate already dead as orality, and that the transcription is carried out with the sorrow of farewells and of the reading of testaments: *post mortem*.

Against this paradox it should be said that when the scribe's ink dries, this is not the exhaustion of a vital force which leaves nothing but an eternally frozen trace. The written *text* lives an *other* life; it is not the enfeebled life of an oral *performance*. Writing has its own proper vitality and opens the text to new adventures. Certainly, Amadou Hampâté Bâ's *Kaïdara* speaks to us of a *Kaïdara* transmitted through memory and through Fulfulde language and cosmogony; but above all it speaks to us of the readings that the French text bearing this title allows, the cosmogonies to which it gives birth, and the new adaptations it permits, which are demonstrated by its many theatrical adaptations.

The same thing is even more true of Birago Diop or of Bernard Dadié. It is important to insist on a point which these writers speak of infinitely less than they demonstrate in their texts: the *pleasure* they take in writing. Indeed, it is with pleasure that orature is welcomed into writing, that the spoken word is reprised, extended, transformed, becomes imprinted with another rhythm: it is not the thought of loss or death that is the principle of this reprise, but that of life, of the power to fabulate – to borrow the word Senghor used to speak of Birago Diop's art. It is agreed too quickly that sub-Saharan African is the domain *par excellence* of what, in opposition to Jack Goody's expression 'graphic reason', the Senegalese philosopher Mamoussé Diagne has called 'oral reason'.[125] In identifying Africanity and orality in an essentialist manner, many end up supporting the view that African literature is only authentic if something in its writing shows that it is still, in some way, marked, as if with a seal, by orality. Or, again, if it shows that it is nothing but the shadow cast by the true Reality, which is naturally oral.

It is time to put an end to the discourse about a griot whose speech would always be found crouched somewhere underneath the writer's. Amadou Koumba, whose name appears on the two collections of 'tales' attributed to him as their 'true' author or at least co-author, is not someone apart from Birago Diop himself: he is a creation of his writing, which is to say that he exists by and for it. To see things this way means understanding that it is time to think about the delight of writing celebrated naturally by writers in their practice, even those who assert the opposite: who identify with an orality whose nostalgic heirs they claim to be, or who declare their regret at having to write in a language they would like to pretend is still foreign to them, while every letter they trace presents it with their greatest possible declaration of love.

Philosophy and Orality

Here, on this precise point concerning orality, is the place to return to Hountondji's criticism of ethno-philosophy. This criticism can be summarized as asserting that one cannot speak of philosophy in the absence of a written tradition; that in a culture of orality the need to memorize and to conserve is so pressing that it leaves no place for the critical examination of the content transmitted; and that, in the final analysis, to posit the equivalence of philosophy and of a worldview expressed in orality would be to accept and even praise the value of unanimity, which would go against the most basic sense of philosophical questioning.

Many of Hountondji's critics have seen in this a discrediting of orality that recalls the thesis that 'societies without writing' are 'inferior' societies, characterized by lack and incompleteness, and have chosen to attribute this to a Eurocentrism and an elitism on the part of the Beninese philosopher: he was seen to have embraced, too hurriedly, a 'Western' conception of philosophy. The Senegalese philosopher Mamoussé Diagne has chosen to examine this important issue concerning orality in the central chapter of his work titled *De la philosophie et des philosophes en Afrique noire* (Of philosophy and philosophers in sub-Saharan Africa).[126]

'Hountondji', he writes, 'the author who has perhaps most frequently evoked the thematic of writing and orality, has, it must be admitted, faced only tentative ideological refutations that leave the serious questions he raised intact'.[127]

Diagne declares that he is sorry that Hountondji did not actually test out his thesis concerning the impossible orality of philosophy through a close examination of 'African traditional thought', and he argues that what he calls 'the method of dramatization' is 'a fundamental characteristic of civilizations of orality'.[128] This dramatization, according to the Senegalese philosopher, is a method that 'Plato the director' often used in his *Dialogues*, and in a similar way, in oral transmission it fulfils an essential 'psychagogic' function. This is because it allows for a loosening of the continuous effort of retention that Hountondji believes is orality's great and permanent concern, meaning that 'the mind', as he writes, 'is too preoccupied with *preserving* knowledge to find the freedom to *criticize* it'.[129]

On the question of knowing if a critical self-relation is possible in oral discourse, I return to a point I have emphasized elsewhere: it is important for us to understand the specific manner in which 'the Tradition [can] be a reevaluation of itself, can become self-criticism'.[130] This requires us to recognize the existence of another process at work: *intertextuality*. Ode Ogede has remarked that criticism in general lacks an essential key to reading African literature as long as it ignores the role played by intertextuality.[131] He calls on critical readers to fully take into account the 'hidden dynamic' of literary creativity on the continent whereby 'African writers alter one another's styles while drawing from older texts to fashion new ones'.[132] Ogede is right, and not only when it comes to literature: to understand orality is to understand that it too involves intertextuality, which is to say the art of producing a text (it makes no difference if this text is oral) in relation to another one, which the new text evokes in different ways: by citing it, making allusion to it, imitating it, miming it, subverting it, treating it at times with derision. In this way orality returns on itself, becoming a critical reworking of its own stories, and along with them the knowledge and values that they can carry and transmit:

it produces new stories that put the old ones, often established as canonical, into question.

For example, there are myths or tales considered canonical that stage a competition between suitors at the end of which the happy victor receives in reward the hand of a young lady. This type of text, which we find across all cultural regions, is canonical in that it is the expression of values held by the society. The detour via a contest only consecrates the one whom everything in the story already designates, and so also consecrates the social norm establishing the matrimonial strategies through which the society perpetuates itself, and which are recognized as one of its pillars. The bow that only Ulysses' arm can bend designates him as the only possible husband for Penelope.

But it so happens that other stories are produced which subvert this one. The 'tales' collected by the anthropologists Philippe Couty and Jean Copans[133] seem to be scabrous stories, scatological and bizarre, as long as they are considered by themselves and not in relation to the canonical form of the story of the suitors that they evidently re-perform as mockery: the contest to determine the happy chosen one might be, for example, a farting contest. And in the volume, every story is of that kind. Because they overlook this dimension of intertextuality and so of parody, however evident it may be, Couty and Copans contort themselves trying to explain why these stories make their audience laugh, and trying to sort out how they reflect the Murid society of Baol where they were produced. If these fake tales have something to say, it is to be found above all in their raising the question of what transformations must have taken place in the society to make it smile that way at the values which, up until then, were the foundation of the matrimonial strategies to which it gives its blessing.

We could also refer to the story 'Penda', which the Senegalese writer Ousmane Socé Diop has a character in his novel *Mirages de Paris* tell in its entirety and which constitutes, in a 'serious' register this time, a subversion of the same myth of the suitors. Here the capricious Penda, a child raised inside the cocoon of all manner of beautiful stories, decides she does not want a fiancé who has a scar. This clear refusal of virile, even of warrior, values of which the scar is a sign, radically questions the destiny that society has written for its girls. Penda pushes her insistence and refusal to the limit and marries the man, without a scar, of her choosing. She is, of course, punished; the chosen one turns out to be a monster from whom she manages to escape with the miraculous help of an old enchanted horse. But in the process she disguises herself as, and then is actually transformed into, a man, a metamorphosis that can be read as signifying her revolt, asserting her determination to decide, as men do, what she wants for herself. Even though she is defeated, according to the moral of the story, she, like Kate, Shakespeare's 'tamed shrew', would have made her own voice exist beneath the dominant discourse, beneath the canonical story.

To sum up – what is known as 'tradition' itself replies 'yes' to the question of whether it is possible to think philosophically, that is to say in a critical and removed fashion, from within orality. The intellectual history of Africa will be written through reflection on cultures where oral transmission is essential, but where criticism, that is to say self-criticism, is not absent, as long as we know where to look for it – in intertextual relations, for example. It is essential, but not exclusive. This intellectual history, and with it the history of philosophical practice in Africa, also cannot be written in ignorance of another tradition, this time a written one, of which the legendary city of Timbuktu, among others, bears witness.[134]

Meanings of Timbuktu

Timbuktu, today, is at the centre of numerous research programmes studying manuscripts, written in the Arabic language and script, in Africa south of the Sahara, of which the American historian John Hunwick has been a tireless pioneer. We are therefore in the process of reconsidering what an article in a French weekly has accurately called 'the external gaze that confines Africa to its oral tradition'.[135] This 'external gaze' is the de-historicizing one that anthropology has long cast on the continent. It has received internal support, Jean-Michel Djian tells us, from 'the significant influence of griots, who maintain oral tradition and oppose evidence of a written tradition in the history of the African continent'.[136] Whether or not it faces open opposition from traditional oral historians, it is time to leave what we could call a *griot paradigm* that identifies Africa with orality, in order to envisage a history of (written) erudition in Africa.[137]

It must be said that the debate over the existence of an African tradition of philosophical thought, and of its possibility in the absence of writing, is often carried out in complete ignorance of the established history of intellectual centres in Africa where texts containing an undeniable philosophical dimension were studied and commented on, in writing, and where the names of Plato and Aristotle, for example, were well known long before the European presence. This ignorance in turn reproduces that of an *other* history of philosophy, found too often among university philosophers, that going beyond its Hegelian reconstruction and canonization should take full account of the paths and detours by which it travelled into regions other than the European continent.

Accordingly, in the African field, it is necessary also to study Islamic philosophy, or more accurately philosophy in Islamic lands, of which Djenné, Timbuktu, Coki (in Senegal) and other sites of erudition in West Africa were repositories.[138]

To begin, then, a brief word on philosophy in Islam, referred to as *falsafa*, a term formed by the Arabization of the Greek *philosophia*. The term *translatio studii* (or *studorium*) has been used to designate the movement that transmitted Greek knowledge and philosophy in the Syriac language and then in Arabic, which was one of the consequences of the closure, in 529, of the different 'pagan' schools of philosophy in Athens and Alexandria by the emperor Justinian. This forced many philosophers to flee from his religious zeal, some of whom found refuge in Persia or on the borders of what today is Turkey. *Translatio studiorum* therefore refers to the way in which Hellenism (philosophy in particular) found itself transplanted into cities like Nishapour, Gundishapur, Edessa, Harran

(Carrhes), and so on, before its flourishing in Baghdad, founded in the middle of the eighth century as the capital of the Abbasid dynasty. In the ninth century the Islamic world's appropriation of Greek philosophy, for the most part Aristotelianism and Neo-Platonism, was carried out under the name of *falsafa*, initially in the form of translations (from Syriac and then directly from Greek). Philosophers referred to themselves by the name *falâsifa* (sing. *faylasûf*). The most celebrated of these were Al Farâbî in the ninth century, Ibn Sînâ (or Avicenna) in the tenth, Al Ghazâlî in the eleventh, and Ibn Rushd (or Averroes) in the twelfth. We should note that although he certainly wrote important philosophical works, Al Ghazâlî was also the author of virulent attacks against the *falâsifa*, whom he accused of heresy, writing from the standpoint of a conservative theologian, which he had taken on in his official role as censor. Since then it has been common practice to identify him with opposition to philosophy on the grounds that it is too rationalist an activity not to be a threat to religion. It is certainly an exaggeration to make Al Ghazâlî solely responsible for the disappearance of a philosophical curriculum in the Sunni world after the thirteenth century (the Shiite world remained, for its part, committed to teaching a Neo-Platonism into whose language Imamism had found a translation). Nonetheless, this disappearance is a reality, even if philosophical thought never ceased to be present in disciplines considered more immediately 'Islamic', like theology, commentary, mysticism or law.

The expansion of Islam in Africa also signified the development of these 'Islamic' disciplines on the continent. In effect, one of the consequences of the Islamization of West Africa, which became significant after the year 1000 C.E., was the introduction of what the anthropologist Jack Goody has called the 'graphic reason' of Islam. He notes that, by reason of its natural link to religion, 'writing was at first valued more for its role in superhuman than in human communication'.[139] Accordingly, he continues, only in the 'long-established Islamic centres' like those of 'Mopti and Timbuktu' was writing used in teaching and study. These centres, he notes, were themselves 'a link with the Mediterranean world ... through the movement of books and scholars'.[140]

Here an important clarification should be made: when these intellectual centres blossomed in the fourteenth century, the great period of development of *falsafa* was over. It therefore would not become a self-standing discipline in Timbuktu and elsewhere. Without making assumptions about the results of inventorying and cataloging of manuscripts in Arabic or Arabic characters – a task that still largely remains to be done – we can wager that there will be few texts that explicitly classify themselves in this discipline or under this label. But, once again, philosophical questions, approaches, or references will be found in texts on theology, jurisprudence, or Sufi metaphysics, all sciences that were studied at Djenné, Timbuktu or Coki. Classical logic in particular (which is to say Aristotelian logic, with elements of Stoic logic) always remained an important component of the curriculum because it was considered an instrument (*organon*) for all the other sciences. Its religiously licit character is still asserted, often while making reference to Al Ghazâlî, on the grounds that this science of the forms of valid reasoning, in contrast to physics or metaphysics for example, contains nothing that could enter into explicit conflict with the religious text. Al Maghîlî's *Rajaz* or the *Sullam al murawanaq* (The Book of Luminous Ascent) by 'Abd Rahmân al Akhdarî (1414–46), both authors from the Maghreb, were pedagogical works on Aristotelian logic extensively used in the different intellectual centres of the continent. It is interesting to note that these texts were written in verse to facilitate memorizing the rules of logic they presented, as if it were necessary in some way to re-oralize the written in the interests of pedagogy.

When a Moroccan military expedition put an end to the Songhay empire in 1591, the consequences of the siege of Timbuktu included the deportation of Ahmad Bâba Al Timbukti al Sanhadjî (1556–1627), an eminent member of the city's intellectual elite, to Morocco. He then spent fourteen years among the scholars of Marrakech, teaching there and so testifying to the quality of the intellectual centre where he had been educated, in particular by Moussa Baghayogo, whom he called 'the master of us all and our protector'.[141] Timbuktu could bear comparison with the finest centres in Morocco and elsewhere in the Muslim world, even if books were rarer – which is why Ahmad Bâba was able, despite everything, to find benefit in an exile that gave him easier access to what had been written in the disciplines that interested him.

We could examine, for instance, one of Ahmad Bâba's works that has been edited, translated to French, and published as *La gratification des hommes de bien par l'exposé des mérites des ulama* (The gratification of men of good will by the demonstration of the merits of the 'Ulama).[142] It proposes a typically classical argument affirming the superiority of the pursuit of wisdom over all other ends. The argumentation is, certainly, based on references to the Qur'an, prophetic tradition, and the authority of recognized scholars, and the conclusion of the work is inspired by Al Ghazâlî's views on its theme, the search for wisdom. Everything Timbuktu represents, its importance for today's Africa, can be expressed by Ahmad Bâba's echo of a saying that is one of Islam's essential messages: more precious than the blood of the martyrs is the ink of the scholars.

Attention to the traditions of erudition in centres like Timbuktu is not only necessary for writing the intellectual history of the continent. It also usefully sheds light on the project of making spoken languages into languages for African modernity. The Muslim scholars wrote mainly in Arabic, but not exclusively. They also used Arabic characters, with adaptations, for texts written in their own first languages. For instance, following the example of Othman dan Fodio (d. 1817) himself, the scholars of the sultanate he created in Northern Nigeria developed a rich literature in Hausa and Fulfulde.[143] Those who are today engaged in the task described in Kwasi Wiredu's slogan as 'Let's philosophize in our languages' would also do well, while engaged in this new *translatio studiorum*, to be aware that their project has a tradition, established by the West African literati whom Ousmane Kane has called 'non-Europhone intellectuals', of which they should be the inheritors.

Socialisms and Democracy

[D]riving home to the masses that everything depends on them, that if we stagnate the fault is theirs, and that if we progress, they too are responsible, that there is no demiurge, no illustrious man taking responsibility for everything, but that the demiurge is the people and the magic lies in their hands and their hands alone.

Frantz Fanon[144]

In November 1976, the Senegalese Progressive Union (l'Union Progressiste Sénégalaise, UPS), the party of Léopold Sédar Senghor, President of Senegal at the time, joined the Socialist International and changed its name to become the 'Socialist Party' (Parti Socialiste). The left-wing opposition quickly started calling it, mockingly, the P'S', putting the word 'socialist' in quotation marks to undermine the socialist credibility of Senghor and his party. What was the significance, in historical and in conceptual terms, of challenging the philosopher of Negritude's socialism?

Senghor's personal history contains nothing to cast doubt on his socialist engagement, which began during his time in *khâgne* in the early 1930s,[145] when he joined circles that identified themselves with this movement. Under the influence of his classmate and friend Georges Pompidou, it seems, he then joined the Republican and

Socialist Students' League of Action (Ligue d'Action Universitaire Républicaine et Socialiste, LAURS). There he met, among others, Pierre Mendès France and Edgar Faure.[146] His engagement deepened when he joined the party of the Senegalese political figure Maître Lamine Guèye (1891–1968), a branch of the French Section of the Workers' International (Section Française de l'Internationale Ouvrière, SFIO), in 1946. That same year, he and Guèye became Senegalese members of the French Parliament. Two years later, he broke with his mentor to create his own party, the Senegalese Democratic Bloc (Bloc Démocratique Sénégalais, BDS), which in 1957 became the Popular Senegalese Bloc, whose fusion with the Senegalese Socialist Action Party (Parti Sénégalais d'Action Socialiste, PSAS) gave birth, in 1958, to the UPS. After the African Assembly Party (Parti du Rassemblement Africain, PRA) joined it in 1962, the UPS gave itself single party status until 1974 when, as much out of personal philosophical disposition as under the pressure of circumstances and of opposition forces, Senghor decided to return to the political pluralism that had been the tradition of the Senegal of the Four Communes.[147]

If the reference to socialism was a constant through all the metamorphoses of a party that finally called itself simply 'socialist', then what about the concept itself? It had been, Senghor explained, his search for a truly African socialism, one that would not be the sheer extension of French socialism in the colony that led him to break with Lamine Guèye's SFIO. This also explains why on his 'left', among the partisans of a socialism that saw itself as scientific, which is to say 'universal', the 'socialist' character of the PS born in 1976 was held in suspicion and so rendered in quotation marks. This search for an 'African' socialism has made up the largest part of political philosophy in Africa. Its main theoreticians were the Tanzanian Julius Nyerere, the Ghanaian Kwame Nkrumah, and, of course, the Senegalese Léopold Sédar Senghor, all of whom were inclined towards the question of socialism's universality in relation to its particular, concrete realizations, here and there.

The African Path to Socialism According to Nyerere

In 'Uhuru na Ujamaa', 'Freedom and Socialism', Julius Nyerere declared:

> The universality of socialism only exists if it can take account of men's differences, and be equally valid for all of them. And it can.... It is my contention that socialist societies in different parts of the world will differ in many respects even when they are fully developed instead of being, as now, at different stages on the road to socialism. The differences between these societies will reflect both the manner of their development, and their historical traditions.[148]

The theorists of African socialism were in deep agreement in their insistence that the plurality of paths to socialism were not in opposition to its universality, but were perhaps even its condition. We can hardly even speak, Nyerere insists, of *an* African path to socialism, since pluralism is also *intra*-African. On this point he writes:

> Indeed, even to talk of 'African' socialism is something of a misnomer. As Africa has been organized into nation states, and because these nation states have been differently developed, there will even be variations of African socialism.[149]

This insistence on beginning from facts on the ground, those of nation-states which, as Nyerere noted, were forged by Europeans over a span of roughly sixty years, bears the mark of the Tanzanian leader's pragmatism.

There is, therefore, a properly Tanzanian socialism, whose Swahili name is *ujamaa*. But, Nyerere adds, we should not be too quick to conclude, from the need to qualify and localize socialism, that it has no meaning in itself or that it is a vague concept. On the contrary, it cannot be separated from the requirement of universality, and there are values and characteristics that define a socialist society and distinguish it clearly from a non-socialist society. Consequently we can, according to Nyerere, establish the elements of a socialist ideal against which to measure the performance of the countries that claim it. The first element, 'the most central', is that Man is the aim of all social activity. And in 'man', he specifies, we should read 'all humans'. Other elements include the ideas of equality, of human dignity, and of democracy. This last one, he declares, if it is not to be an empty concept, assumes that an end has been put to inequality. Consequently, and this is another constitutive element of socialism, the society must be a society of workers where no one is permanently unemployed: this might be attained through a policy of education followed by a return to the soil, for example. There also must be no major income gap, a sign that the society is not based on exploitation. The form of public property can vary, but the principle must be the people's control over the means of production and the mechanisms of exchange. Nyerere also declared forcefully that it is not true that private property cannot exist, nor that persons cannot enjoy individual rights: on the contrary, he said, socialism should be identified with the 'rule of law'. Ultimately, in the socialist society, consideration accorded to an individual will correspond to the measure of his or her service for the public good.[150]

This enumeration of points should not be seen as an attempt to extract a base, a 'common denominator' that would make up the universality of socialism, to which other particulars, belonging to the country in question, would be added in order to characterize this or that road to socialism. To the contrary, the whole text of socialism should be considered to be present there, while the plural paths are so many *translations*, because the relation between the universal and the particular is just this: translation. Nyerere insists that socialism should not be treated as a given, incarnated in a model that then could be repeated: only translations exist, without a text that could be claimed as the original one, written in a sacred language. China, Scandinavian countries, or Israel, wrote Nyerere, are each translations against which to measure the one that would make up an African path to socialism. This one will be all the more original since in Africa socialism does not need to be invented: the humanist philosophy expressed in different African cultures suggests it almost naturally, and the elements that constitute it are found in them, the same ones he had enumerated.

Nyerere added that 'socialism should be secular'. By this should be understood that it does not get involved in the question of adhesion to a system of belief, but that it also does not identify itself with atheism. In effect, he notes, socialism will always 'try to enlarge freedom, and religious freedom is an essential part of man's liberty'.[151] Nyerere also called, firmly and as a matter of course, for non-violence, explaining that although socialist institutions can certainly be imposed by revolutionary violence, the same cannot be said for socialist *attitudes* that alone can give life to these institutions.[152] Generally, for the man whose title was *mwalimu* (the master teacher), education is essential to socialism, above all to make clear the need to go beyond the racialist simplification to which the anti-colonial struggle could lead, presented as Blacks against Whites, and to guard against thinking that it is adequate to replace White or Brown (Asian) capitalists with others who would be Black.[153]

Socialism, Consciencism, Spiritualism and Secularism

Under the name of 'Consciencism', the Ghanaian Kwame Nkrumah also wanted to think out a socialism that would be 'a new emergent ideology... which can solidify in a philosophical statement, but at the same time an ideology which will not abandon the original humanist principles of Africa'.[154]

His approach rests on the notion that philosophy is and should be an ideological instrument that can be used to impress an orientation onto society. Evidently, philosophy can be studied by concentrating on the unfolding of 'chains of reasons' that it contains. But, Nkrumah says, while certain 'Western' philosophers might engage themselves in this contemplation of their civilization, an approach which, he writes, 'emasculates' the discipline by making it lose 'its arresting power', a non-Western student of philosophy, and particularly an African, will have no excuse to see in philosophy anything but the choice with which he is confronted: that of oppression or, on the contrary, of social progress. It is worth citing this central passage from Nkrumah's work in its entirety:

> however dessicated the new passions of some Western philosophers are, they can admittedly claim to share a continuity with a European cultural history. A non-Western student of philosophy has no excuse, except a paedeutic one, for studying Western philosophy in the same spirit. He lacks even the minimal excuse of belonging to a cultural history in which the philosophies figure. It is my opinion that when we study a philosophy which is not ours, we must see it in the context of the intellectual history to which it belongs, and we must see it in the context of the milieu in which it was born. That way, we can use it in the furtherance of cultural development and in the strengthening of our human society.[155]

Before turning to the meaning of Consciencism, we should pause on this assertion that a certain distance ought to be kept from a philosophy 'which is not our own', and that it should be used only as an instrument. We can note that this injunction to 'the non-Western student of philosophy' involves adopting the construction, in the nineteenth century, of the history of philosophy as an exclusively Western adventure: Nkrumah accepts the idea of philosophy as the property of Europe, its unique *telos,* as Husserl would say. We should not then be surprised, in light of his endorsement of instrumentalism, to see him summing up the works of philosophy from 'Western civilization' in rapid formulas, conveniently packaged, and which ultimately say very little. So he says that 'Leibniz's philosophy contributes to a democratic capitalism', while 'in the philosophy of Descartes support is given to co-operative socialism', the reason being that Cartesianism rests on the idea 'that *fundamentally* we are *equally* able to perceive and appreciate the *same* truths'.[156]

These kinds of gross simplifications generally characterize the chapter of *Consciencism* titled 'Philosophy and society', which is concerned with showing that 'there is a *social contention,* implicit or explicit, in the thought of the philosophers, the history of philosophy'.[157] In other terms, that philosophy is, in Althusser's famous formula, 'class struggle in theory'. This is in any case probably inevitable for any attempt to carry out a review, in just a few pages, of many philosophers who lived in different periods, in an attempt to illustrate a general proposition.

The final chapter of the work, the bizarre attempt at a 'mathematical formulation of the system', appears for its part to be a useless tribute to the idea that using a symbolism and set of procedures that imitate mathematical language and proofs is a guarantee of rigour and irrefutability. It is enough to look at the passage translating ideas into symbolic language to see that it lacks any formal coherence that might lead to any necessarily applicable principles.

Ultimately, the presence of this final chapter is even more unfortunate since the book's main proposition defining 'philosophical consciencism' has no need for this gratuitous formalism. What is this proposition? In conformity with the thesis that philosophy is an instrument or ideology at the service of social construction, the central thesis is compounded: first, it affirms that 'it is materialism, not idealism, that in one form or another, will give the firmest conceptual foundation to the restitution of Africa's egalitarian and humanist principles'; and second, since materialism is allied with a socialist philosophy, that this latter is also needed, and therefore that 'the restitution of Africa's humanist and egalitarian principles of society requires socialism'.[158]

Nkrumah shares with Nyerere, and also with Senghor, as we will see, the conviction, which is at the root of each of their political philosophies of an African socialism, that the continent's cultures are traditionally characterized by an egalitarian humanism that makes the collectivity into a veritable *community*; and that, in consequence, the march towards socialism of the postcolonial African nation-state continues the movement by which African societies became communities, as individuals learned to become *persons*. *Becoming a person* and *forming community* are then, it could be said, the two faces, individual and collective, of the same movement.

For Nyerere and Senghor, both believing Catholics, the idea of community has a strong religious resonance. The former insists that what he calls by the Swahili name *ujamaa* carries a sense of 'human fraternity', and the latter reads into it the notion of 'communion'.[159] At root, their respective political philosophies are at least as involved in a Christian reading of Marxism as in a reconstruction of African 'tradition'.

They are then in clear opposition with Nkrumah's socialism, which wanted to base itself on a materialism which, breaking with the usual identification of Africanity and spirituality, he makes the very foundation of the continent's egalitarian humanism. Here the ontology of vital forces on which many African religions rely is to be understood from a materialist perspective: vitalism is materialism, and so is 'philosophical consciencism', defined by Nkrumah as the harmonious synthesis of African traditions of thought and the contributions of Islam and the West. Nkrumah accordingly writes that 'matter is not just dead weight, but alive with forces in tension. Indeed, for the African, everything that exists, exists as a complex of forces in tension. In holding force in tension to be essential to whatever exists, he is, like Thales and like the philosophical consciencists, endowing matter with an original power of self-motion; they were endowing it with what matter would need to initiate qualitative and substantial changes'.[160]

Nkrumah, whose biography tells us that he tried to be both a Christian and a Marxist socialist 'without contradiction',[161] in fact tried to think through to its final implications a 'scientific' socialism that would incorporate African traditions of thought all the more easily because they already anticipated it, including its materialism. If he declares that 'philosophical consciencism, even though deeply rooted in materialism, is not necessarily atheistic', he does so just after having written that 'the affirmation of the sole reality of matter is atheistic, for pantheism, too, is a species of atheism'.[162] There is certainly a contradiction here, and declaring it absent is consequently only a means, pragmatist through and through, of accounting for religion as a 'social fact', which 'must be understood before it can be tackled'. This is because, Nkrumah continues, 'to declare a political war on religion is to treat it as an ideal phenomenon, to suppose that it might be wished away'.[163] Consequently, one must begin from the fact that religiosity results directly from the state of poverty in 'Africa, Asia, Latin America and among the people of African descent in America and the Caribbean',[164] in order to understand that the best course is to insist on the secular character of the state while guarding against presenting this secularism as hostile to religion.

If Nkrumah's socialism aims to be materialist, Nyerere's and Senghor's is spiritualist. Religion inspired Nyerere's political philosophy. This man for whom the Catholic Church, which he converted to at the age of twenty, opened a beatification process in 2005, first of all saw the division of humans into the very rich and the very poor as a scandal, something that shocks the moral conscience. For the pressing reason that the goal of the Church is the human, it has a duty to recognize its own values in the ones claimed by African socialism. All the same, like Nkrumah, he insisted on the need for a secular state. The pragmatic concerns behind this were evident: it was essential not to transform the religious differences in Tanzania (between Christians and Muslims) into political divisions. But it is also clear that all of Nyerere's pluralist philosophy argues in favour of a secularism that it would be responsible to protect. Beyond this, Nyerere affirmed that the values shared by all the major religions, in particular that of the equality of all humans, should be at the foundation of a socialist philosophy.

For Nyerere then, the choice of socialism was ethical more than, as it was for Nkrumah, 'scientific'. According to Senghor, the African path to socialism ought to be equally a realization of African humanism and of Marxist humanism.

Senghor and Humanist Socialism

In 1948, the same year as the publication of the *Anthology* which Sartre's flamboyant preface transformed into a manifesto of *Négritude*, Senghor published an article in *La Revue socialiste* titled 'Marxism and humanism'.[165] This followed the publication of the philosophical writings that Marx had abandoned to the 'gnawing criticism of mice' but had then been rediscovered. These *Manuscripts of 1844* presented a Marx more profoundly Hegelian, a moralist Marx, a Marx, in a word, who put at the heart of his reflection the question of metaphysics and of humanism that could be formulated this way: 'what should be done so that man will no longer be a stranger to himself and to other men?'[166]

In 'Marxism and humanism' the Senegalese philosopher based his definition of humanism on that of Jacques Maritain:

> humanism ... tends essentially to make man more truly human ... by allowing him to participate in everything that can enrich him in nature and history (by 'concentrating the world in man', as Scheler would say, and 'by expanding man in the world'); it demands at once that man develop the virtualities he contains, his creative forces and the life of reason, and that he work to make the forces of the physical world the instruments of his freedom.[167]

It is in light of this definition of *integral humanism*, as Maritain called it, that Senghor examines 'the question of Marx's humanism', which 'was never truly posed until ... the publication of certain works of his youth'.[168] This question, according to Senghor, lost its centrality because Marx, giving in to positivism, set himself to creating a Marxism that would be 'scientific' and where, in particular, the sense of the veritable scandal of man's alienation gave way to the mathematics of the extraction of surplus-value. He acknowledged that in the works after 1851, 'concrete economic and political solutions' were most important to Marx. It was against this development of Marx's maturity that Senghor declared: 'We are not Marxists, we are socialists.'

All the same, said Senghor, the first Marx, according to him the true one, never ceased to be present, hidden at the centre of the so-called mature works. In the end, these were still ultimately concerned with the human struggle against what negates man and which Senghor calls, following Lukàcs, *reification*. They remain concerned with the movement by which man's humanity emerges from petrification. And in what name is this struggle carried out, in what name can this movement go beyond reification, if not in the name of human interiority?[169] In the name of what, if not an exigency that remains ethical through and through? Here we could evoke Mao's famous declaration that the numerous principles on which Marxist theory is founded can all be brought back in the final analysis to a single phrase: it is right to rebel. The first Marx persists in the Marx that follows the 1844 *Manuscripts* because it is Marxism in its totality that calls 'Time for outrage!' in the name of the human.

It also, Senghor tells us, calls 'Time for outrage!' in the name of God because, he explains, behind the issue of the human there is also that of God. Of course, there is the famous formula that declares that religion is the 'opium of the people'. And it is also the case that 'the religious act is [for Marx] the most absolute act of reification'. But Senghor sees in this a 'reaction of Christian origin against the deviations of historical Christianities'.[170]

In consequence, Christianity itself would be well advised not to neglect looking for the God of justice in this reaction, where it might be able to recognize itself. Senghor remarked that 'the most considerable publications of recent years on Marxism itself have been authored by Jesuits'.[171] He is referencing here above all Father Pierre Bigo, whose main work, *Marxism and Humanism*, published in 1952, bears the same title as the article Senghor himself published in 1948. Senghor saw his own political philosophy of a humanist and African socialism fitting into the intellectual movement of social Catholicism that also produced the school that called itself 'Economy and Humanism', founded by the Dominican Father Louis-Joseph Lebret (1897–1966), which taught, the Senegalese poet said, the meaning of an 'open socialism'.[172]

'Open' is the important word here. In his 1948 article, Senghor insisted on the fact that Marxism is a humanism since it is opposed to all fixity. It calls man, as Maritain said, to the development of his creative forces and so, we could add, to his *becoming-person*. We know that for Senghor African philosophies shared this ideal of *becoming-person*: for them 'the 'vital forces' constitute the fabric of a world … animated by a dialectical movement'. This movement is towards the creation and continual reinforcement of a collective that is a community of persons, that is a community precisely because it is made up of *persons*. 'Community' is therefore a central concept that refers at once to African communitarianism and to the Christian ideal; this ideal which is not, for Senghor, absent from Marx's work. And so he agrees with Father Bigo in thinking that there is, in the end, something tragic in the way that Marx was able to 'express a thought so inherently metaphysical and even religious, while repressing the idea of transcendence that it implicates'.[173]

The Democratic Turn and the African Charter on Human and People's Rights

In an article titled 'The "democratic turn" in contemporary African philosophy', Pieter Boele Van Hensbroek observes that 'African political thought changes radically at the end of the 1980s. Socialism, the key political idea since the launch of "African socialism" in its different versions during the 1960s, abruptly disappeared from the intellectual scene…. New flares appeared on the political horizon: they were called democracy, social movements, and civil society'.[174]

No doubt, indeed, socialism was in question, as it was everywhere in the world after the crumbling of 'real socialism', and above all, it should be added, in an Africa that during those same 1980s was being administered the potion of structural adjustment and neoliberal anti-state doctrine. But the socialist ideal, that is to say socialism as an ideal, had not so much disappeared as it had been looking for itself. The Senegalese philosopher Sémou Pathé Guèye, up until the end of his life, never stopped working on the 'project of a philosophy of globalization', one of whose dimensions was precisely the search for a socialism open to democracy, which today has become 'a universal requirement for all peoples, and demands to be endlessly consolidated and deepened, leading to the conquest of new rights ever richer in humanity'.[175] On the philosophical level, this search should lead to a socialism enriched by all the socialisms, beyond the old oppositions between 'scientific', 'utopian', or 'African'. Guèye, who was a significant figure in the communist opposition to Senghor, never doubted that the socialist ideal would be re-founded, as he thought it needed to be, on the basis of what he called a 'return in force of the Ethical', and through the revisiting, among other things, of the 'problematic of the "Civilization of the Universal" developed by thinkers like Father Pierre Teilhard de Chardin and Léopold Sédar Senghor'.[176] On the practical, political level, the stakes of this search were a necessary recomposition and reunification of the African left around an open, ethical socialism, attached to the universal demand for democracy and human rights.

It was this demand that, according to Van Hensbroek, appeared forcefully at the end of the 1980s, with its inaugural moment being the Beninese National Conference which established, at the start of the 1990s, the model for carrying out democratic reforms in different African countries. Accordingly, in the important work he dedicated to the different 'national conferences' held in a large number of Francophone countries during this period, during what he called 'the heights of democratic effervescence',[177] Fabien Eboussi Boulaga speaks of the 'Beninese invention'.[178] While the 'African independences', he explains, had been 'the ratification and the renewal of a regime of heteronomy'[179] created by colonization, the national conferences, marked by the 'undefinable grandeur of beginnings'[180] brought to Africa – and certainly also to political philosophy on the continent – an 'illuminating power … such that, in the present and the foreseeable future, all juridical and political order must begin from the universal principle that follows from it: the need to establish trust and to base freedom in civilization'.[181]

That this African new democratic beginning meant the establishment of a new juridical and political language in the present and for the future was the understanding and wish of the African people who revolted against oppressive single-party regimes. Many also posed the question of how the African past might be transposed into this new language. The authoritarian powers that had governed abusively up until then thought they could find legitimacy in an African 'tradition' of consensus that they claimed was realized in the single party and its leader. Certain African philosophers nonetheless believed that this derailing of tradition should not prevent thinking, today, about an African translation and appropriation of democracy.

A first example is that of the Cameroonian philosopher Jean-Godefroy Bidima, who proposed rethinking today, for the future, the African idea of *palaver*.[182] Writing seven years after the National Conference of Benin, he presented a much more sceptical point of view on what had been accomplished in those grand meetings between the 'living forces' of the Nation, as well as on the way in which these meanings had been analysed. Bidima deplored, in particular, that 'during these national conferences, the critical relation to tradition was not broached, smothered as it was by the settling of scores between intellectual, industrial, juridical, and religious elites' and that *palaver* was poorly imitated by these 'sovereign national conferences¼ whose great weakness was talking exclusively about the state'.[183] He criticized Eboussi Boulaga's reflections and Jean-François Bayart's analyses for their focus on the state. 'African society', he wrote, 'is only an ancillary thought within a general reflection on state power – but should one not follow the model of *la palabre* and reunite in a single reflection the problems of power and those of authority?'[184] This is precisely what his book proposes: to convey the need to rediscover the spirit of *palaver* so as to better develop, going beyond the discourse on the democratic state that was to follow the neocolonial state, a 'local justice' in which populations could recognize themselves and, in a general fashion, (re)constitute a genuine public space:

> In renewing the spirit of *palabre*—rather than the form, since African society changes—Africans will reacquaint themselves with the virtues of this principle of publicity. The fact remains that the tribal model has already realized what contemporary African states are still incapable of achieving: a public space of discussion.[185]

Another example of the search for an African appropriation is the way in which the Ghanaian Kwasi Wiredu encourages the construction in Africa of democracies that will continue its traditions. This seems to turn its back entirely on the very idea of a modern democracy: he sidesteps the demand, which had been at the heart of popular claims, for the end of the single-party regimes and the institution of a multiparty system that gives a meaning to democratic choice. Kwasi Wiredu sees in this nothing but an agonistic conception, a democracy of competition, which he believes a democracy of consensus should oppose. In a perspective that recalls the idea that the Rousseauist general will cannot sustain factions, Wiredu puts the dictatorial regime of the single party and the multiparty regime back-to-back. Writing the political chapters of his book *Cultural Universals and Particulars: An African Perspective* at the start of the 1990s, Wiredu, as a witness of 'the recent wave of multiparty democratic reform in Africa',[186] investigated the merits of this political system. To begin with, he writes, in the countries where it makes up the established tradition, the United States or the United Kingdom for example, we do not see it functioning in a manner 'such as to cause any careful observer to swoon with admiration'.[187] In addition and above all, this system that rests on a political division between a majority that has power and an opposition that competes for it may turn out to be disastrous: 'opposition is still not infrequently seen on both sides as veritable war, with verifiable casualties', Wiredu writes.[188] Sadly, there are examples to support his claims. Because the 'murderous identities' of ethnicity or religion too often become important factors, we can come to fear elections for the violence they can provoke, which may lead as far as to civil war. What Wiredu advocates, therefore, is a democracy without parties, so that there will not be a minority that loses because a majority wins. One could well ask if this is attainable. Wiredu imagines that he has been presented with the following objection:

> It may be conceded that consensus is a beautiful thing, but it cannot be achieved often enough to provide a basis for any practical system of democracy. Perhaps, in traditional times

some African peoples were generally able to reach consensus in their political deliberations, but the conditions of life and economy in those circumstances most likely did not engender issues as acutely divisive as those that bedevil modern life. For example, the kinship basis of representation probably obviated the ideological polarities inherent in the modern party system. But there is, objectively, no returning to that uncomplicated approach to politics. Thus, while the majoritarian system may, in the abstract, be less than the ideal, all the realistic alternatives may be worse.[189]

The Ghanaian philosopher's response to this serious objection he makes to himself consists, on a negative plane, in repeating that the struggle for representation can be deadly if it answers only to the mechanism of the machines for conquering and guarding power that political parties are. On a positive plane, he evokes the example of the Akan traditional system whose spirit, he indicates, can be rediscovered, showing how to avoid a situation where those who have been selected on the basis of ideas that they have debated with others subsequently remain inside a group logic. In this way the elected representatives would give a mandate to the leaders to act in such a way that the administration put in place would reflect, as much as possible, all opinions: it would, in brief, allow everyone to participate.

It is true that multiparty democracy favours populism. It is also true, as Wiredu's imagined objector says, that all the alternatives to this system are to be avoided. Should, then, as an article of the Senegalese constitution stipulates for instance, political parties be forbidden from identifying with a race, an ethnic group or a religion?[190] (We can see here the caution of a legislator who wants an ideal world where adhesion to a party is not the mechanical translation of an ethnic or a religious appurtenance, or both.) Or, on the contrary, should total freedom of expression and association be allowed that would, for example, permit the existence, as is the case elsewhere, of parties called 'Christian democrats'?

These questions should be thought over, particularly that of the relation between ethnicity and citizenship. This is not only an African issue, but it takes a particular importance on this continent due, among other things, to the history by which its nation-states were formed. The 'liberal' democratic vision of things would have citizenship completely separated from ethnicity, the first providing a representation of society made up of abstract individuals, detached from their different belongings in so far as they interact in the public sphere. The most democratic 'communitarian' vision, for its part, calls for realism and insists on the impossibility of such a separation. This second way of seeing things insists on the utopian character of an ethno-culturally neutral citizenship and recalls, for instance, that the conflicts that have regularly reoccurred in the oil-producing region of the Niger Delta since the 1990s, whose actors have been local populations, multinational oil companies, and the Nigerian central state, have shown that citizen mobilization is often also inseparably cultural and ethnic. It could be concluded from this that we must at least ask if ethnicity is not *also* a form of citizenship (rather than its opposite), and so perhaps draw from it positive consequences for the way of imagining a politics of living together within pluralism, ethnic or religious.[191] Here *palaver*, or the politics of consensus, *reinvented* (rather than truly *rediscovered* in African traditions that are themselves always reconstructions in the present and for the present), will certainly play an important role in addressing the important questions concerning the solidity and continuity of the initial social contract, prior to the choices of proper political orientation, in which the competition between values around which parties are formed is also just as necessary.

The struggles that produced 'the wave of democratic reforms' that Wiredu discusses, along with what we call today the 'Arab spring', declare that the demand for multi-party democracy is universal. Bidima and Wiredu's reflections also remind us that the universal exists only in its concrete translations. Political philosophy in Africa is and will be this labour of translation for the construction of an African citizenship.

Conclusion:
Lessons from the African Charter on Human and Peoples' Rights

Let us conclude with this idea of the translation of the universal by addressing the question of translating human rights, as it has been posed on the African continent.

Today, a document, The African Charter on Human and Peoples' Rights, bears witness to the process by which the continent has progressively emerged from its state as a region 'abandoned by human rights', to borrow an expression used by the Senegalese jurist Benoît S. Ngom. I have lamented elsewhere that African philosophers have not 'been much interested in [this] Charter ... which, henceforth, is one of the most important documents produced by the African Union to be opposed ... to the human rights violations which would occur on the continent'.[192] It has in fact 'been jurists, for the most part, who have responded, and with some success, to the urgent demand of making Africa a region where the rights of the person will be at home, as they ought to be everywhere, universally'.[193] The discussions around this Charter, however, have revolved around defining *the* African philosophy of human rights, particularly with regard to the relation of the individual to the community.

The dictatorships that established themselves here and there throughout the continent after independence tried to establish legitimation through a *raison d'Etat*, compounded by a *raison de culture* The *raison d'Etat* was, as discussed earlier, that on the one hand the construction of the nation required a single party headed by a leader in whose hands all power was concentrated to keep the fragile social fabric from being torn apart by identitarian rivalries, and on the other, to set the country on the path towards development along which all its energies, they declared, needed to be unidirectionally channelled. The *raison de culture* stated that African tradition – clearly an invented one – decreed that the individual must always be at the service of the community, in turn represented by the Father (of the nation).

The paradox was that such a *raison de culture* could find support in the theories of philosophers and other African intellectuals who repeatedly declared that 'We [i.e. Africans] put less emphasis on the individual and more on the collectivity, we do not allow that the individual has any claims which may override that of the society. We assume harmony, not divergence of interests, competition and conflict; we are more inclined to think of our obligations to other members of our society rather than our claims against them'.[194] Claude Aké, the author of these lines, here opposes an African context and way of seeing to what he considers a 'Western idea of human rights' which he declares 'presupposes a society which is atomized and individualistic, a society of endemic conflict. It presupposes a society of people conscious of their separateness and their particular interests and anxious to realize them. The legal right is a claim which the individual may make against other members of society, and simultaneously an obligation on the part of society to uphold this claim'.[195]

Claude Aké suspected that if Africa was beginning (at the moment when he was writing) to be interested in human rights, this was because 'the authoritarian capitalism of Africa is under some pressure to be more liberal and thereby create political conditions more conducive to capitalist efficiency'.[196]

It is not by chance that thinkers like Nyerere or Senghor – who tried, on the question of the dialectic between individual and community, to develop a philosophy of the person, or more precisely of the individual, who finds support in the community in order to realize her or himself as a person – contributed to the advance of the cause of human rights in Africa. When in 1975 Julius Nyerere opposed the hosting of a summit of the Organization of African Unity by Idi Amin Dada's Uganda, he did this in the name of respecting human rights. The dictatorship of Uganda's strongman should, he believed, not be permitted to represent Africa. It was not possible to be opposed to South African apartheid while at the same time accommodating the violations of human rights going on in Uganda and elsewhere. Ngom judges that this discourse gave an important impetus to the movement for human rights in Africa.[197]

In 1978, an international conference was held in Dakar on 'Development and Human Rights'. Organized by the Senegalese Association of Juridical Studies and the International Commission of Jurists, it emphasized the idea that human rights, far from constituting a diversion from the demands of development, might on the contrary be a condition for it. It was in this spirit that Senghor, the President of Senegal who had endorsed the meeting, decided to present to his colleagues in Monrovia the following year a resolution that he had Judge Kéba Mbaye prepare. This resolution's unanimous adoption led to the drafting of the 'African Charter on Human and Peoples' Rights'.

The words 'and Peoples' were added to the original title, indicating that the final document was the object of a compromise between two visions, each of which called upon 'African philosophy' for support. Some wanted, in the spirit of Claude Aké's statements quoted above, for emphasis to be put on 'collective human rights for corporate social groups such as the family, the lineage, the ethnic group'.[198] The other idea was that it is the individual who is endowed with rights and that, if they are to be truly promulgated and protected, they must not become hostage to group identities or to a *raison de culture*. The 'collectivist' proposition in article 29, paragraph 7 of the Charter can hardly avoid being read along these lines, as potential justification of such a *raison de culture*, when it declares that 'the individual has the duty ... to preserve and strengthen positive African cultural values in his relations with other members of the society, in the spirit of tolerance, dialogue and consultation and, in general, to contribute to the promotion of the moral well-being of society'.

For what is a positive value? Can a value cease to be positive? And who gets to decide? Without doubt practice and reflection will be able, in the future, to resolve the tension that exists between the contrary visions from whose marriage by compromise the Charter was born. For the development of freedom on the continent, this resolution ought to point towards an affirmation of the person as a carrier of rights that can be opposed to oppressive practices she might encounter in 'tradition'. This affirmation can also root itself in a concurrent tradition, according to which nothing is more important than the becoming-person of the human individual,[199] a tradition that allows African cultures simply to *recognize* the Universal Declaration of Human Rights, in the sense that they are able to *recognize* themselves *in* it.

Notes

1. See the acts of the colloquium: B. Bourgeois and J. Havet, eds, 2001, *L'esprit cartésien. Quatrième centenaire de la naissance de Descartes*, Paris: Vrin.

2.. S.B. Diagne, 2001, 'Esprit cartésien et mathématique de l'esprit', in B. Bourgeois and J. Havet, eds, *L'esprit cartésien. Quatrième centenaire de la naissance de Descartes*, Paris: Vrin, pp. 73–81.

3. What the audience could not have known was the intellectual bond I have with Paulin Hountondji, who has clarified the 'question' of philosophy in Africa for many of us.

4. Interview published 2010 in *La Nouvelle Revue Française* 593, p. 166, Paris.

5. Roger-Pol Droit, 2007, *Généalogie des barbares*, Paris: Odile Jacob, p. 19.

6. Diogenus Laertius, at the very beginning of the work he dedicated to the *Lives and Doctrines of Illustrious Philosophers*, echoed the idea, which as Roger-Pol Droit indicates was widespread in his time (in the 'Introduction' to the two volumes of the anthology *Philosophies d'ailleurs 1, Les pensées indiennes, chinoises et tibétaines*, Paris, Hermann, 2009, p. 18), that 'the study of philosophy had its beginnings among the barbarians'.

7. *ibid.*, p. 28.

8. The text of this interview was first published 2001 in Congo in the *Revue africaine de la science de la mission* 14–14, by Hippolyte Mimbu Kilol under the title 'Mudimbe and his methodological quest for excellence. Interview with V.Y. Mudimbe on the occasion of his 60th birthday'. It has also been collected in a volume of contributions edited by Alphonse Mbuyamba-Kankolongo, *Hommage à Valentin Yves Mudimbe: Pour un nouvel ordre africain de la connaissance*, Paris: Paari, 2011.

9. *ibid.*

10. Lucius Outlaw writes, '"Africana philosophy" is the name for an emergent and still developing field of ideas and idea-spaces, intellectual endeavors, discourses, and discursive networks within and beyond academic philosophy that was recognized as such by national and international organizations of professional philosophers, including the American Philosophical Association, starting in the 1980s. Thus, the name does not refer to a particular philosophy, philosophical system, method, or tradition. Rather, *Africana philosophy* is a third-order, metaphilosophical, umbrella-concept used to bring organizing oversight to various efforts of *philosophizing*—that is, activities of reflective, critical thinking and articulation and aesthetic expression—engaged in by persons and peoples African and of African descent who were and are indigenous residents of continental Africa and residents of the many African Diasporas worldwide. In all cases the point of much of the philosophizings has been to confer meaningful orderings on individual and shared living and on natural and social worlds while resolving recurrent, emergent, and *radically* disruptive challenges to existence so as to survive, endure, and flourish across successive generations'. Outlaw, Jr., Lucius T., 'Africana Philosophy', *Stanford Encyclopedia of Philosophy*, Edward N. Zalta, ed., available at http://plato.stanford.edu/entries/africana/

11. See Shamil Jeppie and Souleymane Bachir Diagne, eds, 2008, *The Meanings of Timbuktu*, CODESRIA and HSRC. See also the work that John Hunwick has dedicated to African literature in Arabic script: *Arabic Literature of Africa*, Leiden: E.J. Brill (6 volumes published between 1994 and 2004).

12. See Mamoussé Diagne, *Critique de la raison orale*, Karthala, 2005, and *De la philosophie et des philosophes en Afrique noire*, Karthala, 2006.

13. Séverine Kodjo-Grandvaux, 2011, 'Vous avez dit " philosophie africaine "?', *Critique* 771–72, August–September, special issue 'Philosopher en Afrique'.

14. See Lewis Gordon, *Existentia Africana: Understanding African Existential Thought*, New York: Routledge, 2000, and *An Introduction to Africana Philosophy*, Cambridge: Cambridge University Press, 2008.

15. Two examples of such works: Kwasi Wiredu, ed., 2003, *A Companion to African Philosophy*, Oxford: Blackwell; F. Abiola Irele and Biodun Jeyifo, eds, 2010, *The Oxford Encyclopedia of African Thought*, Oxford: Oxford University Press.

16. See the interview with Lewis Gordon 'Philosopher en Afrique', published in the special issue of *Critique* edited by Souleymane Bachir Diagne, 771–72, August–September 2011, pp. 626–28.

17. [The French phrase 'la force de vivre', the title of this chapter, can be used colloquially, implying something like 'the will to live'. The English translator of Tempels' *Bantu Philosophy*, the text that sets off Diagne's discussion, translates it and its cognates as 'vital force'. I use 'life force' and similar to keep the colloquial – non-philosophic – tone, and to maintain more distance from the Bergsonian notion of 'élan vital', which may translate Tempel's term but should not be considered identical. – Translator's note.]

18. Bontick, François, *Aux origines de la philosophie bantoue. La correspondance Tempels-Hulstaert (1994-48)*. Translated from the Dutch and annotated by François Bontinck, Kinshasa, Faculté de Théologie catholique, 1985, p. 66.

19. Tempels, Placide, *Bantu Philosophy*, translated by Colin King. Paris: Présence Africaine, 1959.

20. In his excellent biography of Alioune Diop, the creator of the journal and then of the publishing house *Présence Africaine*, Phillip Verdin tells us that 'it was in order to distribute this book ... that Alioune came to create *Présence Africain* as a publishing house'. He adds 'It had turned out to be impossible to find a publisher for a book dedicated to Africa that didn't talk about safari, politics, or apologetics'. (In *Alioune Diop, le Socrate noir*, Paris: Lethielleux Groupe Desclée De Brouwer, 2010, p. 199.) After its first edition was published in 1945 by *Le Lovania* in Elisabethville and Katanga, *La philosophie bantoue* was the first book that Présence Africaine published after its founding in 1949.

21. [*évolué* was a colonial-era term used to refer to colonial subjects who had taken on some of the cultural attributes of Europeans – Translator's note.]

22. Mamoussé Diagne notes that the 'the figure of the Belgian missionary Tempels was privileged' even though he had written his major work almost ten years after the discussions around which the *Négritude* movement would organize. 'In fact', he writes, 'it has come to function as the paradigm of origin, origin not in the chronological sense, but in the theoretical and philosophical sense ... it cannot be ignored that discussions on the existence or non-existence of an African philosophy regularly returned to his work as an unavoidable reference'. *De la philosophie et des philosophes en Afrique noire*, Paris: Karthala, 2007, p. 15.

23. In this case it was the Baluba of the Congo.

24. Césaire, *Discourse on Colonialism*, translated by Joan Pinkham, available at http://www.rlwclarke.net/theory/SourcesPrimary/ CesaireDiscourseonColonialism.pdf

25. Alioune Diop, ''Niam M'paya ou la fin que dévorent les moyens', preface to *La philosophie bantoue, op. cit.*

26. *Bantu Philosophy*, p. 25 [I have altered the English translation (from the French), which softens the colonial tone significantly – Translator's note.]

27. *ibid.*, p. 24.

28. Tempels specifically mentions the revolts in February 1944, especially in Elizabethville.

29. *ibid.*, p. 91. [translation modified]. Tempels adds that one can still check to see if the observation was correctly carried out and if the deductions are valid.

30. Paulin Hountondji writes: 'In writing *Bantu Philosophy*, Tempels aimed to refute the thesis of prelogicality that, directly or indirectly, gave to Black people, as to all those labelled primitives, an excessively negative image. Tempels opposed to the adventurous theses of Lévy-Bruhl and his disciples the thesis, generous in a certain way, of a *sui generis* rationality that could be easily reconstituted, and that claimed the right to the label "philosophy"', preface to Mamoussé Diagne, *De la philosophie et des philosophes en Afrique noire*, Paris: Karthala, 2007, p. 6.

31. We should remember, too, that Lucien Lévy-Bruhl himself, around the same time, retracted his early theses on prelogicality.

32. Bergson, 1935, *The Two Sources of Morality and Religion*, translated by R. Ashley Audra and Cloudesley Brereton, New York: Henry Holt & Co., p. 120.

33. *ibid.*, p. 121. Bergson's emphasis.

34. Descartes, 'Meditations on First Philosophy', translated by John Veitch, in *The Rationalists*, New York: Anchor Books, 1974, p. 133.

35. Jacques Bouveresse, 1982, *L'animal cérémoniel, Wittgenstein et l'anthropologie*, Paris: Éditions L'Age d'Homme, p. 92.

36. Ludwig Wittgenstein, 1953, *Philosophical Investigations*, translated by G.E.M. Anscombe. Oxford: Blackwell Publishers Ltd, p. 82e.

37. W.V.O. Quine, 1976, 'Carnap and Logical Truth', in *The Ways of Paradox, and Other Essays*, Cambridge: Harvard University Press, p. 109.

38. Antoine Berman, 1992, *The Experience of the Foreign: Culture and Translation in Romantic Germany*, translated by Heyvaert, Albany: SUNY Press.

39. Wittgenstein, 'Remarks on Frazer's *Golden Bough*', available at https://docs.google.com/document/d/194Uc_W4nTMjJ6yzfV7WFVuY74zPhcivsam3EqijatXA/edit

40. Berman, *op. cit.*, p. 4. [translation modified].

41. Advocating for his countryman, Leo Apostel demanded that those who, like Fabien Eboussi-Boulaga, '[consider] Tempels' intentions to be those of a representative of a colonial, force, making a last ditch attempt to save a colonial system, preventing real political liberation by means of an alienated ideological liberation' (Léo Apostel, *African Philosophy: Myth or Reality?*, e: Story-Scientia, 1981, pp. 52–53), pay attention to the rest of Tempels' life: the opposition he experienced from the colonial administration and from his superiors, who forced him to leave Africa, and his dedication in establishing the doctrinal and initiatory movement *Jamaa*, whose theology, he said, was 'a radical *pluralism*' (p. 56) At any rate, to reduce the enterprise of 'understanding' the Bantu to the single meaning of a colonial 'ruse' is to oversimplify the relation between colonial knowledge and power by declaring the first to be always in the service of the second. Especially in the case of missionary 'scholars', a will to finding good 'translations' and to dialogue aimed towards conversions to Christianity was a task that often led to their own 'conversion' towards the other.

42. François Bontick, *op. cit.*, p. 59.

43. Césaire, *op. cit.*

44. Apostel, *op. cit.*, pp. 26–29. I cite Apostel's presentation of these axioms word for word, extracted from the commentary that surrounds them.

45. *ibid.*, p. 26.

46. *ibid.*, p. 46. 'Muntu' signifies the human person, and, following the grammar of the indicated languages, its plural would be '*bantu*'.

47. Apostel casually notes the 'ontological and quasi Nietzschean nature' of this ethical conception. He could as easily have evoked Spinoza, whom Nietzsche sometimes hailed as his predecessor.

48. See L.-V. Thomas and R. Luneau, 1969, *Les religions d'Afrique noire. Textes et traditions sacrées*, second volume, Paris: Fayard.

49. *op. cit.*, p. 11.

50. Paulin Hountondji's name in particular has become attached to the critique of the tradition inaugurated by Tempels, which he called 'ethnophilosophy'. See *African Philosophy: Myth and Reality*, translated by Abiola Irele, Bloomington: Indiana University Press, 1996; *The Struggle for Meaning: Reflections on Philosophy, Culture, and Democracy in Africa*, translated by John Conteh-Morgan, Columbus: Ohio University Press, 2002.

51. Tempels, *Bantu Philosophy*, p. 101 [translation modified].

52. No. 5, 1948, pp. 755–60.

53. *op. cit.*, p. 756.

54. *op. cit.*, p. 757.

55. The thesis was published the following year, with the same title, in the Collection des Mémoires de l'Académie Royale des Sciences d'Outre-mer, Brussels (Volume XII, I).

56. Alexis Kagamé, 1976, *La philosophie bantu comparée*, Paris: Présence Africaine, p. 7.

57. *ibid.*

58. 'We start', she writes following Humboldt, 'from the primary and unavoidable fact of the plurality of languages'; 'Philosophizing in languages', *Nottingham French Studies* 49 (2), 2010, p. 18.

59. Cassin, ed., *Vocabulaire européen des philosophies. Dictionnaire des intraduisibles*, Paris: Le Seuil/Le Robert, 2004; *Dictionary of Untranslatables: A Philosophical Lexicon*, Princeton University Press, 2014.

60. Cassin, 'Philosophizing in languages', p. 26.

61. *ibid.*, p. 22.

62. Cassin, *op. cit.*, p. 28 quotes Arendt's *Journal de Pensée*.

63. Cassin, *op. cit.*, p. 25 cites Jean-Pierre Lefebvre, 'Philosophie et philologie: les traductions des philosophes allemands', *Encyclopaedia Universalis*, Symposium, Les Enjeux, 1, 1990, p. 170.

64. See Émile Benvéniste, 'Categories of Thought and language categories', an article written in 1958 that became Chapter 6 of *Problems in General Linguistics* (translated by Mary Elizabeth Meek, University of Florida Press, 1971).

65. Bontick, *op. cit.*, pp. 78–79. Fr. Hulstaert concedes for a moment that his initial thesis can be taken as valid: 'In any case, the theory *agere et esse convertuntur* (action and being are mutually convertible) is held by many European philosophers who oppose it to the overly scholastic *agere sequitur esse* (action follows being). My philosophical colleague says that a thing is in so far as it acts, and that it acts in so far as it is. Being and action are only two aspects of the same reality that our limited intelligence cannot condense into a single thought. The axiom *agere sequitur esse* is based on that. So this colleague agrees with your people' (*ibid.*, p. 83).

66. *ibid.*, pp. 54–55. Tempels seems to be thinking of Christ's words in John 10:10, which Fr. Hulstaert mentions in another letter: *veni ut vitam habeant et abundantius habeant* ('I am come that they might have life, and that they might have it more abundantly').

67. *ibid.*, p. 131.

68. *ibid.*, p. 132.

69. Here we can see 'ethnic' philosophy surpassing itself towards the universal. We can compare this with Wittgenstein's comment on Frazer's insistence on the *strangeness* of the Malay representation of the human soul as corresponding to the body in which it resides. Wittgenstein writes: 'How much more truth there is in this view, which ascribes the same multiplicity to the soul as to the body, than

in a modern watered-down theory.' And adds: 'Frazer doesn't notice that we have before us the teaching of Plato and Schopenhauer.' Wittgenstein, *Remarks on Frazer's Golden Bough, op. cit.*

70. The table is described as follows (see *La philosophie bantu comparée, op. cit.,* pp. 121–22):

MUntu = existent with intelligence (*human*)

KIntu = existent without intelligence (*thing*)

HAntu = localizing existent (*space-time*)

KUntu = modal existent (*way of being of the existent*)

Beyond this, Kagamé tells us, is found 'the Pre-existent, first Cause of Existents, which is not included in the categories'.

71. Nietzsche, *Beyond Good and Evil*, edited by R.-P. Horstmann and J. Norman, Cambridge: Cambridge University Press, 2002, Book I §20, pp. 20–21. This remark is analysed in Marc Crépon's *Le malin génie des langues: Nietzsche, Heidegger, Rosenszweig*, Paris: Vrin, 2000.

72. Kagamé, *op. cit.*, p. 126.

73. Kwasi Wiredu, *Cultural Universals and Particulars: An African Perspective*, p. 107.

74. *ibid.,* pp. 108–9.

75. William Emmanuel Abraham, 1962, *The Mind of Africa*, Chicago: Chicago University Press, p. 111.

76. *ibid.*

77. Along the same lings, Douglas Fraser, in an essay accompanying an exposition of photographs of African art objects organized by the Department of Art History at Columbia University in 1974, wrote that 'African artistic forms ... can equally be interpreted as philosophical observations concerning the nature of the world.' Douglas Fraser, *African Art as Philosophy*, New York: Interbook, 1974, p. 1.

78. *First arts, arts premiers* is now adopted in French instead of the colonial phrase 'primitive arts'.

79. See Souleymane Bachir Diagne, *African Art as Philosophy: Senghor, Bergson, and the Idea of Negritude*, translated by Chike Jeffers, Seagull Books, 2011.

80. Their *La sculpture nègre primitive*, Paris: Ed. G. Crès & Cie, appeared in French in 1929.

81. L.S. Senghor, 1964, 'Ce que l'homme noir apporte', *Liberté I. Négritude et humanisme*, Paris: Seuil, p. 35. Senghor's emphasis.
82. *ibid.*
83. *ibid.*
84. *Liberté I. Négritude et Humanisme, op. cit.*, pp. 211–12.
85. See S.B. Diagne, *op. cit.*, p. 86.
86. In 'Sciences humaines et prévision', 1957; reprinted in Gaston Berger, Jacques de Bourbon-Busset and Pierre Massé, 2007, *De la prospective: Textes fondamentaux de la prospective française 1955-1966*, texts compiled and edited by Philippe Durance, Paris: L'Harmattan, p. 53.
87. *ibid.*, pp. 55–56.
88. cf. Gaston Berger, 'L'homme et ses problèmes dans le monde de demain: Essai d'anthropologie prospective', 1955, in *De la prospective, op. cit.*, p. 33.
89. [An English-language equivalent to Berger's 'prospective' disciplines might be 'forecasting' or 'future studies'; but in the absence of a developed reception of Berger in English, and to keep the resonances the 'pro' of prospective has with other terms in this essay, 'project' and 'projection' in particular, I have used 'prospective' throughout – Translator's note.]
90. *ibid.*, p. 34.
91. On this speech and some of the written responses it solicited, see *L'Afrique répond à Sarkozy, contre le discours de Dakar*, Paris: Philippe Rey, 2008.
92. *Et si l'Afrique refusait le développement*, by Axelle Kabou (Paris: L'Harmattan, 1991) is the title that best expresses this point of view.
93. [The French title, *Quel avenir pour l'économie africaine?* is more overtly future-oriented, and also refers to 'an' African economy – Translator's note.]
94. Jean-Claude Berthélemy, ed., 1995, Whither African Economies? OECD Development Centre Seminars series, Paris: OECD. These lines perfectly echo what, several years earlier, Barber B. Conable wrote in his preface to a World Bank report titled *Subsaharan Africa: from crisis to sustainable growth* (1989). 'Africa's continuing economic crisis', he writes, '*presents an extraordinary challenge* [my emphasis] to

the development community – to both intellectuals and policymakers' (p. xi). For a discussion of Afropessimism in relation to prospective and development, see Souleymane Bachir Diagne, 2000, 'Reconstruire le sens: textes et enjeux de prospectives africaines', Dakar: CODESRIA.

95. In his contribution to the collection *L'Afrique répond à Sarkozy*, the writer Boubacar Boris Diop, who is not often in agreement with L.S. Senghor's theses, wrote 'The poet of Joal was cited several times by Nicolas Sarkozy in laudatory terms. What is most ironic is that, whatever we might think of Senghor, it is not certain that he would have allowed a state guest of Senegal to make such outrageous statements that Thursday, July 26, without giving him some kind of reply. Being a deft politician did not prevent him from having pride and a sense of history' (p. 143).

96. John Mbiti, 1990, *African Religions and Philosophy*, second edition, Oxford: Heinemann. My commentary on Mbiti's text is for the most part an adaptation of my article titled 'On prospective: development and a political culture of time' *Africa Development* 29 (1), 2004, pp. 55–69.

97. Mbiti *op. cit.*, p. 26.

98. *ibid.*

99. Mbiti *op. cit.*, p. 17.

100. Mbiti gives as examples eight months bearing similarly 'poetic' names like 'give water to your uncle' or 'grain in the ear' used by the Latuka. (Mbiti, *op. cit.*, p. 20, note 1.)

101. Mbiti, *op. cit.*, p. 23.

102. Mbiti, *op. cit.*, p. 19.

103. Mbiti, *op. cit.*, p. 27.

104. Joseph K. Adjaye accurately notes that Lucien Lévy-Bruhl is without doubt the author who had the greatest influence on the 'anthropological and philosophical discourses on time in Africa', which he said was nonlinear, 'in contradistinction to the "civilized time" of Westerners'. The primitive spirit is unable to represent to itself a homogeneous time, like a line that the imagination can extend indefinitely, Joseph K. Adjaye, ed., *Time in the Black Experience*, Westport, CT and London: Greenwood Press, 1994, p. 3.

105. See Kwame Gyekye, 1987, *An Essay on African Philosophical Thought: The Akan Conceptual Scheme*, New York: Cambridge University Press.

106. [*avenir*, one of the words used in French to refer to the future, is a conjunction of 'à venir', 'to come' – Translator's note.]

107. Mbiti, *op. cit.*, p. 24.

108. Engelbert Mveng, 1976, 'La conception du temps', *Ethiopiques* 6, available at http://ethiopiques.refer.sn/spip.php?article416

109. *ibid.*

110. *ibid.*

111. Gaston Berger, 1964, *Phénoménologie du temps et prospective*, Paris: Presses universitaires de France, p. 214.

112. *ibid.*

113. *ibid.* p. 212.

114. *ibid.* p. 210.

115. Marcel Griaule, *Conversations with Ogotemmeli: An Introduction to Dogon Religious Ideas*, translated by R. Butler, A.I. Richards and B. Hooke, Oxford: Oxford University Press, 1975, p. 137. The original French text is available at http://classiques.uqac.ca/classiques/griaule_marcel/ogotemmeli_dieudeau/ogotemmeli_dieudeau.html, the quote is on p. 157.

116. The fact that this *cri du coeur* was uttered to the UNESCO tribunal during this international organization's eleventh General Conference in 1960, the year of the majority of African independences, contributed to its dramatic tone it took on.

117. [The *Institut Français d'Afrique noire*, based in Dakar, later renamed the *Institut Fondamental d'Afrique noire* and merged into the Université Cheikh Anta Diop de Dakar – Translator's note.]

118. Abbé Grégoire, 1810, *Enquiry Concerning the Intellectual and Moral Faculties, and Literature of Negroes; followed with an account of the life and works of fifteen negroes & mulattoes, distinguished in science, literature and the arts*, translated by D.B. Warden, Brooklyn: Thomas Kirk, p. 164. Available at http://digital.tcl.sc.edu/cdm/ref/collection/access/id/1325

119. Blaise Cendrars, 1927, 'notice', in *Anthologie nègre*, Paris: Au Sans Pareil.

120. Ralph Austen quotes this interview with Biton Coulibaly. He writes: 'In an interview recorded sometime during the 1970s, Hampâté Bâ indicates the complexity of his relationship to writing and languages: "I think initially in Peul, then transpose my thoughts into French, then I translate my thoughts word by word into French. Afterwards I force myself to put my text into good French ... I get one or more French people to read my text and, if necessary, ask them to suggest corrections".¼ The statement concludes with a revelation that Hampâté Bâ had done considerable writing in Fulfulde, but it was all poetry, mostly religious, and none of it published. These poems were 'mes seules oeuvres de creation¼. Ralph Austen, 2010, 'The Medium of 'Tradition¼; Amadou Hampâté Bâ's Confrontations with Languages, Literacy, and Colonialism', *Islamic Africa* 1 (2), Northwestern University Press, p. 219.

121. L.S. Senghor, 1961, 'Préface' to Birago Diop, *Les nouveaux Contes d'Amadou Koumba*, Paris: Présence Africaine, p. 7.

122. Birago Diop, 1961, 'Introduction' to *Les Contes d'Amadou Koumba*, Paris: Présences Africaine, p. 12. Note that Blaise Cendrars had already, in the 'notice' to his *Anthologie nègre*, lamented the lack of 'fidelity' and 'literary exactness' in the stories 'as the missionaries and explorers brought them to Europe and published them'.

123. Paul Ricoeur, 2006, *On Translation*, translated by Eileen Brennan, New York: Routledge, p. 24.

124. Ricoeur says that what must be given up is precisely 'the ideal of the perfect translation', *ibid.*, p. 29.

125. Mamoussé Diagne, 2005, *Critique de la raison orale: Les pratiques discursives en Afrique noire*, Paris: Karthala.

126. Mamoussé Diagne, 2006, *De la philosophie et des philosophes en Afrique noire*, Paris: Karthala and IFAN.

127. *ibid.*, p. 32.

128. *ibid.*, p. 51.

129. P. Hountondji, 1996, *African Philosophy: Myth and Reality*, translated by Henri Evans and Jonathan Rée, Bloomington: Indiana University Press, p. 103.

130. S.B. Diagne, 1995, 'Sur le caractère littéraire de la littérature orale: Lecture des *Contes wolof du Baol*', in *Komparatistische Hefte* 11, Bay-

reuth, p. 107. Mamoussé Diagne agrees with my presentation of this point, which owes much to his own examination of the meaning of the method of dramatization.

131. Ode Ogede, 2011, *Intertextuality in Contemporary African Literature: Looking Forward*, Lexington Books.

132. *ibid.*, p. ix.

133. Jean Copans and Philippe Couty, 1976, *Contes wolof du Baol*, Paris: UGE.

134. Leo Africanus' account, in his *The Description of Africa*, is often quoted: 'There are in Timbuktu numerous judges, teachers and priests, all properly appointed by the king. He greatly honors learning. Many hand-written books imported from Barbary are also sold. There is more profit made from this commerce than from all other merchandise.' Leo Africanus, *History and Description of Africa*, translated by John Pory, London: Hakluyt Society, 1896, excerpted at http://www.learnnc.org/lp/editions/nchist-colonial/1982

135. Valérie Marin La Meslée, 2012, 'Tombouctou, les trésors de Sankoré', *Le Point, Références* 38, Paris, p. 106.

136. Jean-Michel Djian, 2012, *Les manuscrits de Tombouctou: Secrets, mythes et réalités*, Paris: Lattès.

137. *Tombouctou: Pour une histoire de l'érudition en Afrique de l'Ouest* is the French title of the volume Shamil Jeppe and I put together and whose original English title was *The Meanings of Timbuktu*.

138. I restrict myself here to West Africa, what was known as *Bilâd as Sudân* or Sudân.

139. Jack Goody, 1999 [1987] *The Interface between the Written and the Oral*, Cambridge University Press, p. 137.

140. *ibid.*, p. 129.

141. As reported by Al-Sa'di in his *Tarikh al-Sudan*.

142. Ahmad Bâba, 1992, *La gratification des hommes de bien par l'exposé des mérites des ulama*, edited and translated by Said Sami and Mohammed Zniber, Rabat: Institut d'Études africaines.

143. See Mervyn Hiskett, 1975, *A History of Hausa Islamic Verse*, London.

144. Frantz Fanon, 2004 [1961, French original] *The Wretched of the Earth*, translated by Richard Philcox. New York: Grove Books, p. 139.

145. [*Khâgne*, refers to a two-year programme of study taken after secondary school by students preparing for entry into the *école normale supérieure* for sciences and humanities, at the time the pinnacle of the French educational system – Translator's note.]

146. [Mendès France and Faure were both prominent left-wing French politicians and major figures in the Radical party during the fourth Republic; Mendès France was briefly Prime Minister 1954–55 – Translator's note.]

147. Saint-Louis, Dakar, Rufisque and Gorée were 'communes de plein exercise', meaning their inhabitants, French citizens and not subjects, participated in multi-party elections.

148. Julius K. Nyerere, 1969, *Nyerere on Socialism*, Oxford University Press, p. 29.

149. *ibid.*, p. 20.

150. *ibid.*, pp. 30–35.

151. *ibid.*, p. 40.

152. *ibid.*, pp. 49–50.

153. *ibid.*, p. 56.

154. Kwame Nkrumah, 1964, *Consciencism*, New York: Monthly Review Press, p. 70.

155. *ibid.*, p. 55.

156. *ibid.*, p. 52. These formulas do not say very much, and it is, for example, a misinterpretation of Leibniz's monadology to claim that at times one monad 'luxuriates' at the cost of 'the dimness of other monads'.

157. *ibid.*, p. 53.

158. *ibid.*, p. 77.

159. He wrote that African society is 'communitarian' and that this should be understood to mean that it is a 'communion of souls more than an aggregation of individuals'. (*Nation et voie africaine de socialisme*, Paris: Présence Africaine, 1961, p. 71.)

160. *Consciencism*, pp. 97–98.

161. *Ghana. The Autobiography of Kwame Nkrumah*, Panaf Books, 2002, p. 12.

162. *Consciencism*, p. 84.

163. *ibid.*, p. 13.

164. *ibid.*, pp. 13–14.

165. Reprinted in *Liberté 2: Nation et voie africaine du socialisme*, Paris: Seuil, 1971.

166. Senghor wrote in 'Nationhood', published in English in *On African Socialism*, translated by Mercer Cook, New York: Frederick A. Praeger, 1964, p. 30: 'Alienated from himself, the salaried producer becomes a stranger to other men behind a screen of objective products.... But the alienation in turn affects the employer, who betrays his human nature'. These words echo what he had written in 1948 in 'Marxism and humanism': 'by the fact that he is alienated from himself, man becomes a stranger to man, that is to say to other men.' (*op. cit.*, p. 40.)

167. Senghor, *Liberté 2*, pp. 29–30.

168. *bid.*, p. 30.

169. *ibid.*, p. 55

170. *ibid.*, p. 57.

171. *ibid.*, p. 43.

172. The importance of this School on a practical level in determining the orientations set out for an independent Senegal should be noted, as well as the role played in the planning and development of the country by Father Lebret and his team. In 1951, Father Lebret gave his approval to a book by another major representative of the philosophy of the 'Economy and Humanism' school, Henri Desroche (1914–94). This work, titled *Signification du Marxisme*, was rejected by the Vatican and published by Éditions ouvrières. See Roland Colin, 'L'origine de la formation par la recherche et la recherche-action, sur les traces d'Henri Desroche et de ses compagnons' (The origins of education by research and research-action, following Henri Desroc he and his companions), in *En quête d'une intelligence de l'agir: Practiciens en recherche-action*, edited by Pierre-Marie Mesnier and Christophe Vandernotte, Paris: L'Harmattan, 2012, pp. 13–21.

173. Pierre Bigo, 1961 [1952], *Marxisme et humanisme*, 3rd revised edition, Pairs: Presses Universitaires de France, p. 142.

174. Pieter Boele Van Hensbroek, 2011, 'Le " tournant démocratique " dans la philosophie africaine contemporaine', *Critique* 771–72, August–September, p. 654.

175. Sémou Pathé Guèye, 2000, 'Projet d'une philosophie de la mondialisation' ('Project for a philosophy of globalization'), *Ethiopiques* 64–65. Available via http://ethiopiques.refer.sn

176. *ibid.*

177. Fabien Eboussi Boulaga, 1991, *Les conférences nationales en Afrique noire: Une affaire à suivre*, Paris: Karthala, p. 8.

178. *ibid.*, p. 29. Apart from Benin, Mali, Togo, Niger and the Republic of the Congo all had national conferences. Senegal, for its part, returned in 1974 to its long tradition of multiparty elections (in the four communes of Saint-Louis, Dakar, Rufisque, and Gorée, whose inhabitants were French citizens not colonial subjects).

179. *ibid.*, p. 95.

180. *ibid.*, p. 173.

181. *ibid.*, p. 172. Fabien Eboussi Boulaga deals quickly, with good reason, with the idea that these democratic beginnings had been orchestrated from the outside, or more precisely by France – as if one could invent from the outside what was here the principal cause: the desire of the people for democracy.

182. Jean-Godefroy Bidima, 1997, *La Palabre. Une juridiction de la parole*, Paris: Éditions Michalon. Translated in *Law and the Public Sphere in Africa:* La Palabre *and Other Writings*, translated and edited by Laura Hengehold, Bloomington: Indiana University Press, 2013.

183. *ibid.*, p. 47.

184. *ibid.*, p. 164n. The book Bidima mentions is Jean-François Bayart, *L'État en Afrique, la politique du ventre*, Paris: Fayard, 1991.

185. *ibid.*, p. 34.

186. Kwasi Wiredu, 1996, *Cultural Universals and Particulars: An African Perspective*, Bloomington: Indiana University Press, p. 178.

187. *ibid.*

188. *ibid.* Note that chapter 13 of the book, 'Philosophy and the Political Problem of Human Rights', from where this quotation is taken, was

initially an article published in 1995, just after the genocide of Tutsis in Rwanda.

189. *ibid.*

190. This is in article 4 of the Constitution which declares: 'Political parties ... must respect the Constitution as well as the principles of national sovereignty and democracy. It is not permitted for them to identify themselves with a race, ethnic group, sex, religion, sect, language, or region.'

191. The *General Assembly of CODESRIA* held in Kampala from 8–12 December 2002 allowed for important discussions between African intellectuals around this question, clarified among others in contributions by Wilson Kaplan: 'Identity Mobilization and Conflict in Nigeria's Oil Communities: A "Civic" Appraisal of the "Ethnic"'; and by Dickson Eyoh: 'The Ethnic Question in African Democratization Experiences'.

192. Souleymane Bachir Diagne, 2011, 'Philosophie africaine et Charte africaine des droits de l'homme et des peuples', *Critique* 771–72, August–September, p. 671. I take up certain aspects of this article here.

193. *ibid.*

194. Claude Aké, 1987, 'The African context of human rights', *Africa Today* 34 (142), p. 5. John Mbiti gave the most concise expression of the primacy of the community when he wrote: 'the individual can only say: I am because we are; and since we are, therefore I am' (*African Religions and Philosophy*, p. 106).

195. *ibid.*

196. *ibid.*, p. 7. Pieter Boele Van Hensbroek says that for the branch of Marxist thought which shares this point of view, 'the democratic turn was a provocation' (2011, p. 658), because it also signified the refusal of the view whereby the demand for respect of human rights was an imitation of the capitalist West.

197. He retraces the steps in Benoît S. Ngom, 1984, *Les droits de l'homme et l'Afrique*, Paris: Silex. I am relying here on his description of these different steps, as well on the book by the judge Kéba Mbaye, *Les droits de l'homme en Afrique*, Paris: Éd. A Pedone, 2002.

198. Aké, *op. cit.*, p. 9.

199. I also argue in 'Philosophie africaine et Charte africaine des droits de l'homme et des peuples' that the famous 'Hunter's oath' of the Mandé can perfectly easily be considered a declaration of rights attached to the individual, to the 'life' that the first article of the oath declares: 'all human life is *a* life. It is true that one life comes to existence before another life, but no life is more ancient or more respectable than another life, and in the same way one life is not superior to another life'. See Y.T. Cissé and J.-L. Sagot-Duvaroux, 2003, *La Charte du Mandé et autres traditions du Mali*, Paris: Albin Michel. See also the collective work, *La Charte du Kurukan Fuga: Aux sources d'une pensée politique en Afrique* (*The Charter of Kurukan Fuga: origins of political thought in Africa*], Paris: L'Harmattan, 2008.

Bibliography

Abraham, William Emmanuel, 1962, *The Mind of Africa*, Chicago: Chicago University Press.

Adjaye, Joseph K., ed., 1994, *Time in the Black Experience*, Westport, CT and London: Greenwood Press.

Africanus, Leo, 1896, *History and Description of Africa*, translated by John Pory, London: Hakluyt Society. Available at http://www.learnnc.org/lp/editions/nchist-colonial/1982

Aké, Claude, 1987, 'The African context of human rights', *Africa Today* 34 (142): 5–13.

Apostel, Léo, 1981, *African Philosophy: Myth or Reality?*, Gent: Story-Scientia.

Austen, Ralph, 2010, 'The medium of "tradition": Amadou Hampâté Bâ's confrontations with languages, literacy, and colonialism', *Islamic Africa* 1 (2): 217–28.

Baba, Ahmad, 1992, *La gratification des hommes de bien par l'exposé des mérites des ulama* (translated and edited by Said Sami et Mohammed Zniber), Rabat: Institut d'Études africaines.

Benvéniste, Émile, 1971, *Problems in General Linguistics*, translated by Mary Elizabeth Meek, University of Florida Press.

Berger, Gaston, 1960, 'Méthodes et résultats', *Revue prospective* 6, November, Presses universitaires de France. Available at http://www.prospective.fr/idversionUtilisateur.asp?ID=16

Berger, Gaston, 1964, *Phénoménologie du temps et prospective*, Paris: Presses universitaires de France.

Berger, Gaston, de Bourbon-Busset, Jacques, Masse, Pierre, 2007, *De la prospective. Textes fondamentaux de la prospective française 1955-1966*, compiled and edited by Philippe Durance, Paris: L'Harmattan.

Bergson, Henri, 1935, *The Two Sources of Morality and Religion*, translated by R. Ashley Audra and Cloudesley Brereton, New York: Henry Holt & Co.

Bidima, Jean-Godefroy, 2013, *Law and the Public Sphere in Africa:* La Palabre *and Other Writings*, translated and edited by Laura Hengehold, Bloomington: Indiana University Press.

Bigo, Pierre, 1961, *Marxisme et humanisme*, third revised edition, Paris: Presses Universitaires de France.

Boele, Pieter, 2011, 'Le " tournant démocratique " dans la philosophie africaine contemporaine', *Critique* 771–72, April–September, special issue 'Philosopher en Afrique'.

Bontick, François, 1985, *Aux origines de la philosophie bantoue. La correspondance Tempels-Hulstaert (1944–48)*, Translated from Dutch and annotated by François Bontinck, Kinshasa: Faculté de Théologie catholique.

Bourgeois, B. and Havet, J., eds, 2001, *L'esprit cartésien. Quatrième centenaire de la naissance de Descartes*, Paris: Vrin.

Cassin, Barbara, 2010, 'Philosophizing in languages', *Nottingham French Studies* 49 (2): 17–28.

Cassin, Barbara, ed., 2014, *Dictionary of Untranslatables: A Philosophical Lexicon*, Princeton University Press.

Cendrars, Blaise, 1927, *Anthologie nègre*, Paris: Au Sans Pareil.

Césaire, Aimé, 1972 [1955], *Discourse on Colonialism*, translated by Joan Pinkham, New York and London: Monthly Review Press. Available at http://www.rlwclarke.net/theory/SourcesPrimary/CesaireDiscourse onColonialism.pdf

Cisse, Youssouf Tata and Sagot-Duvauroux, J.-L., 2003, *La Charte du Mandé et autres traditions du Mali*, Paris: Albin Michel.

Collectif, 2008, *L'Afrique répond à Sarkozy. Contre le discours de Dakar*, Paris: Philippe Rey.

Collectif, 2008, *La Charte du Kurukan Fuga. Aux sources d'une pensée politique en Afrique*, Paris: L'Harmattan.

Colin, Roland, 2012, 'L'origine de la formation par la recherche et la recherche-action, sur les traces d'Henri Desroche et de ses compagnons', in Pierre-Marie Mesnier and Christophe Vandernotte, eds, *En quête d'une intelligence de l'agir, Praticiens en recherche-action*, Paris: L'Harmattan.

Copans, Jean and Couty, Philippe, 1976, *Contes wolof du Baol*, Paris: UGE.

Crepon, Marc, 2000, *Le malin génie des langues: Nietzsche, Heidegger, Rosenzweig*, Paris: Vrin.

Descartes, René, 1992, *Méditations métaphysiques*, Paris: Flammarion.

Diagne, Mamoussé, 2005, *Critique de la raison orale. Les pratiques discursives en Afrique noire*, Paris: Karthala.

Diagne, Mamoussé, 2006, *De la philosophie et des philosophes en Afrique noire*, Paris: Karthala.

Diagne, Souleymane Bachir, 1985, 'Sur le caractère littéraire de la littérature orale. Lecture des *Contes wolof du Baol*', in *Komparatistische Hefte* 11, *Voies nouvelles de l'historiographie littéraire*, Bayreuth: Universität Bayreuth.

Diagne, Souleymane Bachir, 2000, *Reconstruire le sens: textes et enjeux de prospectives africaines*, Dakar: CODESRIA.

Diagne, Souleymane Bachir, 2001, 'Esprit cartésien et mathématique de l'esprit', in B. Bourgeois and J. Havet, eds, *L'esprit cartésien. Quatrième centenaire de la naissance de Descartes*, Paris: Vrin.

Diagne, Souleymane Bachir, 2004, 'On Prospective: Development and a Political Culture of Time', *Africa Development* 29 (1) 55–70.

Diagne, Souleymane Bachir, 2011, *African Art as Philosophy: Senghor, Bergson, and the Idea of Negritude*, Calcutta, London and New York: Seagull Books.

Diagne, Souleymane Bachir and Jeppie, Shamil, eds, 2011, *Tombouctou. Pour une histoire de l'érudition en Afrique de l'Ouest*, translated by Ousmane Kane, Dakar and Cape Town: CODESRIA and HSRC.

Diagne, Souleymane Bachir, 2011, 'Philosophie africaine et Charte africaine des droits de l'homme et des peuples', *Critique* 771–72, August–September, special issue 'Philosopher en Afrique'.

Diop, Birago, 1961, *Les Contes d'Amadou Koumba*, Paris: Présence africaine.

Dijan, Jean-Michel, 2012, *Les manuscrits de Tombouctou. Secrets, mythes et réalités*, Paris: Lattès.

Droit, Roger-Pol, 2007, *Généalogie des barbares*, Paris: Odile Jacob.

Droit, Roger-Pol, 2009, *Philosophies d'ailleurs 1, les pensées indiennes, chinoises et tibétaines*, Paris: Hermann.

Eboussi Boulaga, Fabien, 1993, *Les conférences nationales en Afrique noire. Une affaire à suivre*, Paris: Karthala.

Fanon, Frantz, 2004, *The Wretched of the Earth*, translated by Richard Philcox, New York: Grove Books.

Fraser, Douglas, 1974, *African Art as Philosophy*, New York: Interbook.

Grégoire, Abbé Henri Baptiste, 1810, *Enquiry Concerning the Intellectual and Moral Faculties, and Literature of Negroes; followed with an account of the life and works of fifteen negroes & mulattoes, distinguished in science, literature and the arts*, translated by D.B. Warden, Brooklyn: Thomas Kirk. Available at http://digital.tcl.sc.edu/cdm/ref/collection/access/id/1325

Goody, Jack, 1999 [1987], *The Interface between the Written and the Oral*, Cambridge: Cambridge University Press.

Griaule, Marcel, 1975, *Conversations with Ogotemmeli: An Introduction to Dogon Religious Ideas*, translated by R. Butler, A.I. Richards and B. Hooke, Oxford: Oxford University Press.

Guèye, Sémou Pathé, 2000, 'Projet d'une philosophie de la mondialisation', *Ehiopiques* 64–65. Available via http://ethiopiques.refer.sn

Gyekye, Kwame 1987, *An Essay on African Philosophical Thought: The Akan Conceptual Scheme*, New York: Cambridge University Press.

Hiskett, Mervyn, 1975, *A History of Hausa Islamic Verse*, Routledge: Curzon.

Hountondji, Paulin, 1996, *African Philosophy: Myth and Reality*, translated by Henri Evans and Jonathan Rée, Bloomington: Indiana University Press.

Hountondji, Paulin, 2002, *The Struggle for Meaning. Reflections on Philosophy, Culture, and Democracy in Africa*, translated by John Conteh-Morgan, Athens, OH: Ohio University Center for International Studies.

Hunwick, John and O'Fahey, Rex Sean, 1995, *Arabic Literature of* Africa, Leiden: Brill.

Kabou, Axelle, 1991, *Et si l'Afrique refusait le développement*, Paris: L'Harmattan.

Kagame, Alexis, 1956, *La philosophie bantu-rwandaise de l'être*, Collection des Mémoires de l'Académie Royale des Sciences d'Outre-mer, (Vol. XII, I), Brussels.

Kagame, Alexis, 1976, *La philosophie bantu comparée*, Paris: Présence Africaine.

Kilol, Hippolyte Mimbu, 2001, 'Mudimbe et sa quête méthodique de l'excellence. Entretien avec V.Y. Mudimbe à l'occasion de ses 60 ans', *Revue africaine de la science de la mission* 14–14.

Kodjo-Grandvaux, Séverine, 2011, 'Vous avez dit " philosophie africaine "?', in *Critique*, 771–72, August–September, special issue 'Philosopher en Afrique'.

Malabou, Catherine, 2010, 'Entretien', *La Nouvelle Revue Française* 593, April.

Mbaye, Kéba, 2002, *Les droits de l'homme en Afrique*, Paris: Ed. A. Pedone.

Mbiti, John, 1990, *African Religions and Philosophy*, second edition, Oxford: Heinemann.

Mveng, Engelbert, 1976, 'La conception du temps', *Ethiopiques* 6. Available at http://ethiopiques.refer.sn/spip.php?article416

Ngom, Benoît S., 1984, *Les droits de l'homme et l'Afrique*, Paris: Silex.

Nietzsche, Friedrich, 2002, *Beyond Good and Evil*, edited by R.-P. Horstmann and J. Norman, Cambridge: Cambridge University Press.

Nkrumah, Kwame, 1964, *Consciencism*, New York: Monthly Review Press.

Nkrumah, Kwame, 2002 [1957], *Ghana. The Autobiography of Kwame Nkrumah*, Panaf Books.

Nyerere, Julius K. 1969, *Nyerere on Socialism*, Oxford University Press.

OECD, 1995, *Whither African Economies?* Paris: OECD.

Ogede, Ode, 2011, *Intertextuality in Contemporary African Literature. Looking forward*, Lexington Books.

Quine, Willard Van Orman, 1996, *The Ways of Paradox and Other Essays*, New York: Random House.

Ricoeur, Paul, 2004, *Sur la traduction*, Paris: Bayard.

Tempels, Placide, 1948, 'L'étude des langues bantoues à la lumière de la philosophie bantoue', *Présence Africaine* 5.

Tempels, Placide, 1959, *Bantu Philosophy*, translated by Colin King, Paris: Présence Africaine.

Tempels, Placide, 1982, *Plaidoyer pour la philosophie bantu et quelques autres textes*, Preface and translation by A.J. Smet, Kinshasa: Faculté de Théologie catholique.

Senghor, Léopold Sédar, 1961, 'Préface' à Birago Diop, *Les nouveaux Contes d'Amadou Koumba*, Paris: Présence Africaine.

Senghor, Léopold Sédar, 1964, *Liberté I. Négritude et humanisme*, Paris: Seuil.

Thomas, Louis-Vincent and Luneau, René, 1981, *Les réligions d'Afrique noire. Textes et traditions sacrées*, second edition, Paris: Stock.

Verdin, Philippe, 2010, *Alioune Diop, le Socrate noir*, Paris: Lethielleux Groupe Desclée De Brouwer.

Wiredu, Kwasi, 1996, *Cultural Universals and Particulars: An African Perspective*, Bloomington and Indianapolis: Indiana University Press.

Wittgenstein, Ludwig, 1953, *Philosophical Investigations*, translated by G.E.M. Anscombe, Oxford: Blackwell Publishers Ltd.

Wittgenstein, Ludwig, 1982, *Remarques sur le Rameau d'or de Frazer*, traduction Jean Lacoste suivie de Jacques Bouveresse, *L'animal cérémoniel, Wittgenstein et l'anthropologie*, Paris: Editions L'Age d'Homme.

Wittgenstein, Ludwig, 'Remarks on Frazer's *Golden Bough*', accessed at https://docs.google.com/document/d/194Uc_W4nTMjJ6yzfV7WFVu Y74zPhcivsam3EqijatXA/edit

World Bank, 1989, *Sub-Saharan Africa. From Crisis to Sustainable Growth. A long-Term Perspective Study*, Washington, DC: World Bank.

Printed in the United States
By Bookmasters